Changing the Art of **Inhabitation**

Alison and Peter Smithson

Changing the Art of **Inhabitation**

Mies' pieces
Eames' dreams
The Smithsons

Artemis
London Zürich Munich

First published
1994 by
Artemis London Ltd.
55 Charlotte Road,
London EC2A 3QT

British Library
Cataloguing in
Publication
A CIP record for this
book is available
from the British
Library

ISBN 1 874056 37 4
(London)
ISBN 3 7608 8429 6
(Zürich)

Designed by
Jonathan Moberly
Printed and bound
in Hong Kong

Preface

This document comprises edited essays and notes, both published and unpublished, under three titles – <u>Mies' pieces</u>, <u>Eames' dreams</u>, and <u>The Smithsons</u> – thus spanning three generations of modern architects whose thinking and work have changed our art of inhabitation.

1

12 September 1958.

Letter from PS to
AS
Carman Hall,
IIT Campus, 60 East
32nd Street, Apt 16,
Chicago 16.
Postmarked
25 September 1958.

Some notes on what I've seen so far of Mies. Structural steel used as such has a quality that nothing else has, and even its having to be <u>painted</u> seems an advantage.

Aluminium is quite useless for cities; it corrodes away and filthies in about four to six years.

860 Lake Shore Drive[1] (the undoubted Parthenon of Mies) is being repainted, I assume for the first time. The aluminium window frames are being painted grey and the steel black. The result is that original idea is so re-established it can, just, ride-over the additions of fifty types of air-conditioner and blower which have been put into the lower window panel.

This painting business seems to give a solidness and historical existence to things. Boats repainted, no matter how bashed about, look OK. Smart yet not <u>new</u>. Old things cannot look new.

Mies' new black anodised-aluminium blocks next to 860 Lake Shore Drive have the imitation look and already the surface anodising is beginning to peel off in sheets like sunburnt skin.[2,3] So it looks as if even Mies can make <u>Miestakes</u>.

2

3

4

5

Certainly at IIT[4–6] there are many errors. The early buildings in concrete and <u>wood</u> windows (presumably built during the war) and later concrete and steel windows, 1958, are very very Krefeld. Especially as the Campus is dumped in the middle of a slum/industrial area. Krefeld was definitely the starting point and he suppressed both it and those early buildings here. Of course there is so much good – 75 per cent is successful, 10 per cent terrific and the rest somewhat studied and not tough enough for their use. I can't really blame him.

The concrete, brick and aluminium windows [of the building] I am in are really excellent but spoiled by shabbiness which mars the external definition. I have come to the conclusion that it's potty to try and make a building which can get dirty well. <u>We have to do away with smoke from town centres and dwelling areas</u>. It's uncivilised and wasteful of labour and effort not to.

Mies uses concrete blocks in the Harkness Commons building (Union) and then sprays them with a spotty cold glaze (he also cold-glazes inside lifts) which is textured, rough and is tough and easily cleaned. He is an old fox.

6

Summer 1958, PS.

Footnote on the Seagram Building, Architectural Review, December 1958.

No other men have succeeded as have Le Corbusier and Mies van der Rohe in building complete systems. Their concentration is such that the nature of their systems is implicit even in the fragment. One has, for example, a perfectly clear notion of the sort of city and the sort of society envisaged by Mies van der Rohe, even though he has never said much about it. It is not an exaggeration to say that the Miesian city is implicit in the Mies chair.

Le Corbusier's system is of course more familiar because of his constant reiteration of the part even his smallest objects play in his general scheme of things. What validates both their systems is that they are conceived in terms of the technology of their time and that both men have a capacity for rejection and reconsideration in the face of changing circumstances.

375 Park Avenue[7] is a fragment, one feels, of a city of towers. But this city does not exist.What does exist is a corridor street called Park Avenue with its own undeniable 1958 life and therefore some right to continuing existence, or at least revalidating modification. We have to ask: does the fragment communicate the dream, at the same time coming to terms with reality, or does it in any way not meet these requirements either by intention or default?

The building in its uncompleted state might seem to the knowledgeable observer (who had also available the published drawings and photographs of the model), as well as to the ordinary observer, to be a 'dry-stick'. This is due perhaps to a built-in resistance to academic disciplines which are too unsubtle to the professional and too subtle to the man in the street. But Mies has in the past extended neo-classical disciplines far beyond what seemed possible … and of course he has done it again. The symmetry of Seagram seems entirely justified for it quite regenerates the Racquet Club which forms the other side of its piazza.

The Seagram Building certainly communicates

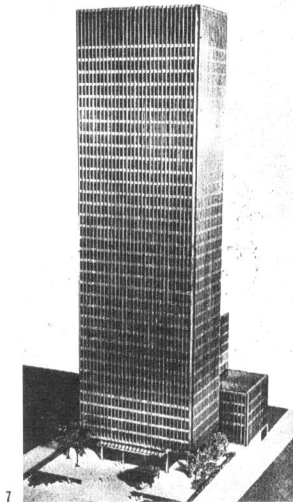

7

8

a dream of a controlled, spacious, <u>machine age</u> environment, even at the popular level, and it faces the issue of coming to terms with the corridor street idea. Its long axis is <u>parallel</u> to Park Avenue and this minimises the destruction of the street which the creation of an open space involves, and its bustle marries it to the cross-streets.[8]

One is however nagged by the idea that the unit of redevelopment is too small for radical space change and that the Rockerfeller Center, which maintains the Avenue frontage and at the same time builds up a new life space behind, is a more real, even more poetic, ideal. But at the same time one cannot deny the fact that Park Avenue is so over-built that it has ceased to have any validity as a street and screams out for pools of calm however they can be got.°

How much of the successful accomplishments of this particular piece of sleight of mind was due to the collaboration of Philip Johnson is a little difficult to assess. Philip Johnson would be the first to give the entire credit for the conception to Mies van der Rohe, but his own house at New Canaan[9] shows that the canon can be, if not transcended, at least dimensionalised; that is, given a feeling of actual rather than abstract existence. One wants to touch it and 375 Park Avenue certainly has this quality.

What faults it does have seem to start behind the external skin. One is worried by an arbitrariness in the relationship between the supporting columns and the mullions seen from the outside, and on the inside they are clumsy in the office space. The inside spaces are fine when they are simple and one can see them outside, but none of the suites of rooms which have been specially designed seems to have any relationship with the fundamental organisation of the building, or to utilise the potential relationship with the outside space and the views. It may be that a Mies building can only really have one sort of internal space.

° Arthur Drexler has written in the <u>Architectural Record</u> of the historical antecedents of the Seagram Tower, but unfortunately his piece seems to have been cut short at the point at which he would, one assumes, have explained how de Stijl and neoclassicism are reconciled. In essence, of course, both are classical aesthetic techniques. The magic of Mies lies precisely in being able to perform this remarkable trick.

9

10

11

12

13

Summer 1959, PS.

In a curious way Mies van der Rohe's work in Chicago has both normality and light-filled poetic space. That work, like Mies, is just what one expects: no more, no less. If 860 Lake Shore Drive[10] is the Parthenon of his steel phase, Crown Hall[11] is his Ephesus. (And there is a whole new period of somewhat disconcertingly chi-chi aluminium/tinted glass anonymity just beginning: 900 Lake Shore Drive, Commonwealth Apartments.[12, 13])

The early buildings on the IIT Campus are technically little improvement on their prototype at Krefeld (the early IIT buildings were built in wartime) and there is a steady improvement in detailing, durability, control of staining and so on, which, as one would expect, parallels the refinement and extension of the formal vocabulary. The Campus is on the whole wearing very well (rather too well in some cases).

The early Promontory Apartments[14] I find crumby; lacking Mies' otherwise never-absent feeling for proportion.

The Carman Hall group[15, 16] is particularly elegant and pleasant to live in. These, like most Mies buildings, are characterised by a feeling of spaciousness and well-being – the space for the social gesture – in the public parts of the building.°

'Chicago and the West'.
Extract probably from a lecture at the Architectural Association School, London; photographs published in Architectural Association Journal, August 1959.

° This feeling reaches an apogee between the pilotis under the Seagram Building, New York – one feels a little timid of actually using the space, as if it were intended for people, if not bigger, at least above one's station.

14

15

16

Sunday, 6 February,
and Thursday, 11
February 1966, PS.

My own debt to Mies is so great that it is difficult for me to disentangle what I hold as my own thoughts, so often have they been the result of insights received from him.

'For Mies van der Rohe on his 80th Birthday', <u>Bauen & Wohnen</u>, May 1966.

I sense, however, that I have been profoundly changed by two themes of his life's work: firstly, that to make a thing well is not only a moral imperative, but it is also the absolute base of pleasure in use; secondly, the machine-calm city – open, civilised, patrician. Mies has hardly ever been interested, even in G days, in machine-age rhetoric. He had a banker's calm, a love of orderliness and quiet built into him.

Mies' thought runs very deep and is not easily accessible – not even one suspects to himself – so the re-direction of the main stream of architecture, which one's instinct tells one lies in his work, will take some years for us to comprehend and to grow upon.

1965–66, PS.

'Without Rhetoric',
extracts from the
text of a seminar
held at the
Technische
Universität, Berlin
(possibly co-
incident with Team
10 meeting, 1965;
Technische
Universität paper,
March 1966;
integrated in
Without Rhetoric,
Latimer, 1973.

One knows instinctively that a reduction of urban densities is a human necessity ... this is why we will return so often to Lafayette Park in Detroit,[17–19] to feel again its decent calm, its openness; to study its methods of putting the car in its place; all achieved without rhetoric ... for us these are the buildings of the hinge-point.

1968–69, PS.

'Mies van der Rohe', based on a seminar held at the Technische Universität, Berlin, 4–9 December 1967; Technische Universität paper, January 1969; Architectural Design, July 1969; integrated in Without Rhetoric, Latimer, 1973.

A building today is interesting only if it is more than itself; if it charges the space around it with connective possibilities – especially if it does this by a quietness that up to now our sensibilities have not recognised as architecture at all, let alone seen clearly enough to isolate its characteristics – to see that it presents us with the new, softly smiling face of our discipline.

It is probably fairly easy to recognise this new face in the gentle, careful façades of the Eames House, but to see it in the equally careful but more coldly ordered façades of Mies van der Rohe's big urban projects is a more difficult step.

Before Mies van der Rohe left Germany in 1938, aged 52, he had already established a kind of modeshift in the discipline of architecture: not that it is always clear. It can be seen emerging in the skin studies of the Friedrichstrasse office building, Berlin (1919); the glass skyscraper (1920–21); the concrete office building (1922). It began to be real in his architecture on the street façade of the apartments at the Weissenhofsiedlung, Stuttgart (1927) and in the layout of the buildings in front of the main factory at Krefeld (1932–33).

Two separate but reciprocal themes emerge: an almost autonomous, repetitive, neutralising skin; and an open-space-structured building – recessive, calm, green, urban pattern. Together they are Mies' immortality.

And there is something else which cannot easily be described – Mies' feeling for materials as luxury, for example the flat, wide rendered wall surface in the Afrikanischestrasse housing[20–22] (1925) brings out the essence of cement rendering as cement rendering and plays a part in the way whereby the ordinariness is raised to a kind of dignity. And, after the uncharacteristic Wolf House (1926), whose bricks are almost sexy, the brick of the Lange House, Krefeld, (1928) is as brick as brick can be – dour, puritan, absolute; representing Mies' attitudes before and after the Weissenhofsiedlung. Before, somewhat rhetorical, influenced by the School of Amsterdam and by

Theo van Doesburg; afterwards, tougher, nearer to Oud.

The luxury rests in the fact that one is aware of the essential <u>thingness</u> of brick and this particular façade is saying 'and that is all you're getting' – a quality seen in an obvious way in the travertine/marble/chromium (nickel) plate/raw silk of the early work and in the Tugendhat House.

In this attitude Mies has been amazingly consistent.

Take an early work, the Perls House,[23, 24] Berlin-Zellendorf (1911). In 1967 it is still recognisable, but the patent prosperity of the small pharmaceutical manufacturing firm who occupy it seems to guarantee that it will not be recognisable for much longer.

The studio part at the rear° seems to have been altered in the 1930s. The main house still has the calm, anonymous rectangular form, good rendering and a creeper which looks as old as the house. All characteristic Mies things. The rhythm of the upper storey, a french window alternating with an ordinary window, reappears at the Weissenhofsiedlung.

According to Philip Johnson this house was designed when Mies was working for Peter Behrens and it is during his period with Behrens (1908–11), when in St Petersburg as supervisor of construction for the German Embassy, that Mies must have had his first contact with the aristocratic tradition of planning.

This tradition of ordered, calm, inviolable open spaces, as an urban tradition, is not as visible in Germany°° as it is for example in India at Jaipur, Delhi, or Agra, or in England at Bath. So it may have been his contact with the expansive spaces and expansive uses by the Neva that turned his mind to an ideal open-space-structured, building-recessive, calm, green, urban pattern. Certainly, in his first actual building after the 1914–18 war, the Municipal Housing in the Afrikanischestrasse, by setting the building back from the road slightly more than usual and by a careful restraint in the

° Not visible in the photograph shown in <u>Mies van der Rohe</u>, Philip Johnson, MOMA, New York 1947.

°° Munich is in the Palazzo tradition, but a little white neo-classical pavilion for 'taking the waters' by Schinkel is in Aachen.

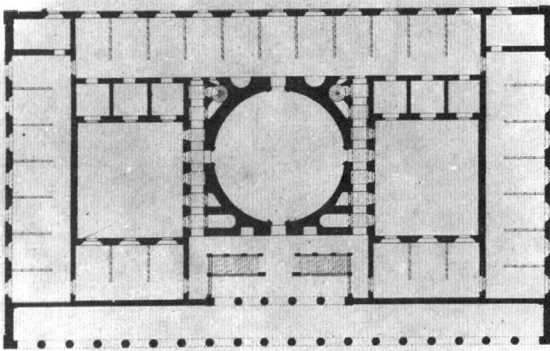

façade design, a more expansive place is established than one would have believed possible with such limited means. The total feel of this place is built up carefully by very simple means – the quiet courts with just grass and trees, the well-proportioned façades, the decent rendering we have spoken of earlier, and the neat brick detail. It has the gentlemanliness that was the beau idéal of Adolf Loos.

One further thing about those days in Berlin before the first war. Today, certainly, the Altes Museen is the only old building in Berlin with an absolute presence. To us it seems one of the great carrier buildings of the nineteenth century – carrier in the sense that it carries the notion of architecture from one century to the next – but as we have been brought to it by Mies' architecture one must be wary. The Altes Museum[25] is a subtly modulated box whose cool corners, as well as the general parti, are very Miesian. In whatever way Mies consciously set about studying it in his Berlin days when he was 19, he took it all in – along with that famous Berlin air – and caught the breath of the possibility of that almost autonomous repetitive neutralising skin that was to be so important to his architecture. Of course the Altes Museum worked on Mies in many more obvious ways as well° and Crown Hall's only real triumph seems to be the production of a version of the museum in the teeth of a practical programme of accommodation.

But in a less obvious way, as we have already said, it influenced him even more. Schinkel used the neutralising skin of columns to enable him to melt away the classic academic problem of where to enter a circular space, but in fact he produced a new sort of building. A compact, carefully modulated package, underplaying the contents, typical of advanced neo-classicism, but dissimilar from earlier classical buildings in which each part is given a distinct form, such as the British Museum.°°

The Altes Museum is a very original work. Mies got the message and it began to creep more and

° The two boxers in black profile in his 1942 drawing of the Fieldhouse at IIT work in an identical way as the two 'Man with Horse' groups on top of the central block of the Altes Museen.

°° By Sir Robert Smirke, 1780–1867, an almost exact contemporary of Schinkel. The British Museum front was built 1823–47. Pevsner: 'Begun 19 years after the Altes Museum was engraved and thus known about.'

26

27

28

29

30

31

more into his work as he got older – see for example how the projecting staircase towers of the original design for IIT were gradually withdrawn behind the skins of the buildings in the built version.

And, to repeat, it was already evident in the garden façade of the apartments at the Weissenhofsiedlung[26] that the façade has become a skin: the proportion of glass to solid has gone up; the glass has become sky-involving, structure-dissolving; the vertical mullions are modulation, marking not mastering. By the time 900 Lake Shore Drive came to be built, the outside of the building had become an almost too autonomous neutralising skin, the necessary concomitant of Mies', by now highly developed, open-space-structured urban pattern.

This open-space-structured urban pattern first became real in his work in the grouping of the outriding pavilion buildings at the Krefeld factory[27] (1932–33) in which are displayed all the formal characteristics – in the buildings, in the layout, in the planting (weeping willows, smooth lawns) – that we are so familiar with from the IIT campus. In some way it was all already there at Krefeld.

At the same time as the Krefeld factory, Mies was building in Berlin the Lemcke House.[28-30] [*] This house is, from the road, pavilion-like and its garden runs down to a small lake with a public park beyond – a setting of quiet within a city, complete with the fisherman in a moored punt and the obligatory weeping willows.

The ideal of a calm, open-space-structured urban pattern as realised at Lafayette Park, Detroit[31] (designed 1955, built 1959 onwards), is a place full of potential and of lessons – in its discreet means of traffic separation, its car/house to-the-whole-city scaled urban structure. It brings into Detroit an amazing other idea of how life could be lived with machines.

In the second stage of the building of Lafayette Park's tall apartment blocks[**] the skins are even more <u>neutralised</u> and the parked motor-cars are kept even more out of sight. (Mies changing the face of changing circumstance and also carrying

[*] In 1966 it was in good condition externally, restored by the State the previous year. The only Mies court house built; L-shaped plan, one studio wing deceptively large, the window strip 6 feet high. Its type-form much used in Hilberseimer's later planning studies.

[**] A gap between the first and second stages was presumably due to the death of Mies' client in an air-crash into the East River, New York.

32

33

34

35

out a kind of private tuning-up of the concept after the experience of the first run.)

Lafayette Park is attributed jointly to Ludwig Mies van der Rohe and Ludwig Hilberseimer. The open-space-structured urban pattern was one of Hilberseimer's life's themes ... it was a vision shared.

The large, at-the-whole-community scale central open-space appears over and over again in Hilberseimer's studies, as indeed did repetition (especially in those competition projects he did before leaving Germany), but repetition in Hilberseimer became obsessive and curiously life-excluding. With Mies, this is never so (or hardly ever).° With Mies, repetition is life-including, his feel for it can make the multiplied thing magical in its very multiplication. This is a knife-edge phenomenon, most easily observable in the restored Stoa of Attalus in Athens.[32]

It would seem in fact as if repetition as a quality in itself (this is a quality that has been misinterpreted as endlessness by critics when they have found repetition used as a formal technique by Mies) is first used consciously in Hellenistic architecture and this reaches us in its most potent visual form (or at least, did, before the Americans rebuilt the Stoa of Attalus) in the precise and beautiful – if aseptic – axonometric drawings of agoras of Greek towns in Asia Minor made by Germans in the period from 1900 to 1940. One campaign of the excavations of Priene seems to have gone on between 1895–98, the results being published in Berlin in 1904, just in time, one is tempted to think, for Mies' arrival there in 1905.

On reflection, a repetitive almost autonomous neutralising skin appears in another architecture; in Italian Romanesque – notably at Pisa (cathedral eleventh century, baptistry twelfth/thirteenth centuries), and in other eleventh-century buildings[33,34] of which the re-build (sixteenth century) in the Piazza San Marco of the Procuratie Vecchia[35] in Venice is a very obvious example. But the phenomenon has never been commented on in the

° Almost always so in Mies' followers.

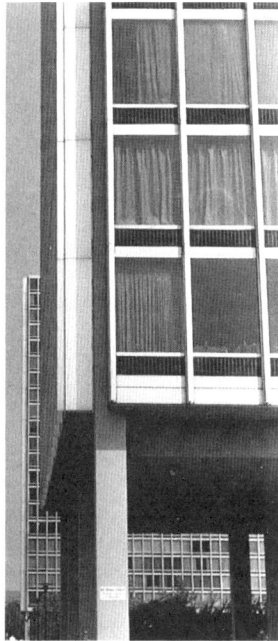

36

37

sense that a well-proportioned bay, when repeated, is magically enhanced, which is, one supposes, part of the 'how sweet is perspective' felt by its inventors in the early Renaissance. In these beautiful Italian buildings it is certainly easy to see that repetition is not a life-excluding concept.

Mies has without doubt moved even more towards the use of repetition because the culture he is working in is particularly good at the quality control of serially-produced, identical, metal objects and, as he has always loved metal, he swims freely in this technology. Not only this, but there is also an American architectural tradition of fine materials and careful detailing, from which he has been able to draw support – for architecture is a collective achievement and cannot be achieved in the teeth of an alien or antagonistic society, or in opposition to the prevalent technology.

Certainly the skin of Mies' Colonnade Apartments[36, 37] (1958–60) would be unachievable outside the world of US technology. He has moved from the poetry of <u>assembled</u> components – the rolled sections and bricks of one of the earliest buildings at IIT, the Metal and Minerals Research Building[38, 39] (1942–43)° to the unique extrusions of aluminium and neoprene of the Colonnade skin. Mies is working through the available technologies and at New Jersey a very high level of formal sophistication is achieved on the same budget as conventional speculative builders' projects.

In the eighteenth century, porticos, pediments and regular ranks of windows – a very narrow vocabulary – were manipulated with considerable variation as <u>signs</u> (a portico for example indicating an entry point). This vocabulary lost formal meaning, but nevertheless people could read the function and the status of the building by subtle signs – about the state of upkeep, the dress of people going about, and so on – and could find their way about all right. It did not lose all meaning to the society using it; far from it, they used it with plea-

° This is the building that captured our interest in Mies when first it was published in England in 1946. It is a wonderfully clear exposition – because the things it is assembled from are humble – of how his handling makes us see their richness.

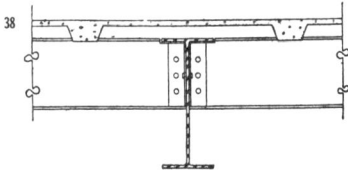

sure. Capacity to detect small differences is very marked in the human sensibility. Mies in his sort of detailing is a precursor, a maker (as is Jean Prouvé) of another sensibility concerning architecture.

Those who think that Mies is 'all the same' or who confuse a sixties Braun toast-maker with a record player, will find that their children, who at seven can date Volkswagens by the small yearly detail changes, do not have these problems, By anyone truly bedded in our culture, a building of Mies can be placed with ease, certainly dated within three years by the dozens of signs to do with changing building technique and the refinement of the formal idea – as easily as a contemporary could have dated a painting by Bellini.

Mies is surprisingly tuned-in to our culture. His Museum of the Twentieth Century in Berlin shows what has really happened since art began to be taken out of houses and churches and put into national collections in the 1820s. Pictures began to be painted especially for the museums and become almost totally dependent on them, in the sense that many present-day paintings are really cult objects needing every bit of presentation, myth-making and commentary they can get. Mies' big-box in Berlin accepts <u>and</u> clarifies what is going on – that art now needs a big reliquary box to sustain it.°

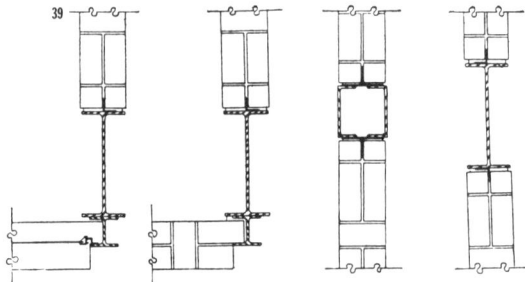

° (See Appendix 1, page 67.)

February 1971, PS.

Ludwig Mies van der
Rohe drawings in
the collection of
MOMA, Ludwig
Glazer, extracts
from book review,
Architectural
Design, May 1971.

Mies was 83 when he died in 1969. In 1935, when he first visited the United States, he would have been 50 – with the greater part of his working life still ahead of him. What should the curators of drawings collections now keep to show how his buildings were thought about and made in this long, second period, of his life?

The drawings one went to look at in Mies' office in the 1950s and 1960s were the working drawings, shop drawings and schedules, for somehow one sensed that in them the secrets and the expertise of the complex later works were to be found. The means of formal control of the art of architecture had changed and changes further.

And would one be wrong in thinking that the 1922 Concrete Office Building[40] – the Mies perspective of which is so buildable, so clear, so new – was really seminal to the Dutch in their heroic period? Or seminal to Van Nelle, to Zonnestraal and the open-air school in Amsterdam? One has to remind oneself, seeing how real this drawing is, that in 1922 there existed of the modern canon only Le Corbusier's Villa at Vaucresson, Oud's Café De Unie, and the small Victor Bourgeois house in Brussels.

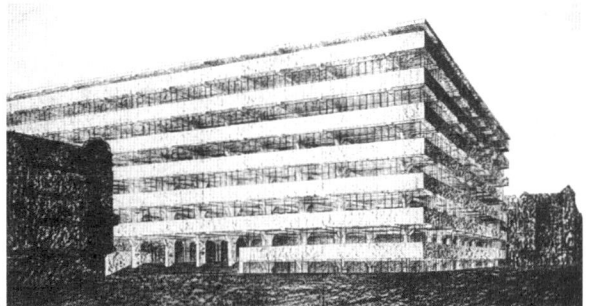

1968–69, PS.

The house of Le Corbusier at Garches … or his   <u>Without Rhetoric</u>,
truly named Maison des Heures Claires at Poissy   Latimer, 1973.
… Mies' staggeringly opulent Barcelona Pavilion
… or his Tugendhat House at Brno … were the Villa
Rotondas of their time.

Undated, AS.

On looking at illustrations of the Werkbund Exhibition of 1914, there would appear certain influences on Mies ...

Hoffmann Pavilion, (Austrian Werkbund Building)
  : is a reminder of East Berlin house (Lemcke)
  : has large window, tall; striped walls
  : has chairs set out against this background
  : has figure sculpture
  : whole effect postulates great influence.

Van der Velde's theatre:
  : again the scale
  : small windows in perfect brickwork
  : big doors
  : one senses a great influence on the Krefeld houses.

Possible influence on Mies of Werkbund Exhibition, 1914. Exhibition demolished in 1915; building in Germany only began again 1922/23; most of the rest of the Exhibition influenced/became the Fascist style. Unpublished.

May 1975, PS.

It was not until the late forties and fifties when Extract from
Mies van der Rohe himself began to underscore 'Making the
the generalised theoretical base on which his work Connection',
was established and growing, and his work itself Architectural
simplified to a point where its underlying organi- Design, May 1975.
sational principles were easily available, that mod- (See also page 139.)
ern architecture as the beginning of an
architecture became recognised. It had been Mies'
intuition that from its isolated Villa beginning modern architecture was capable, by continuous internal invention and enquiry, of becoming the
architecture of the epoch.

In Mies the critical nature of the generalised
ideal is continually stated, especially in his later,
American, years and it is for this reason that there
are followers of Mies – Miesians – in many places
in Europe and the United States of America, as
there were in the past Palladians.

At the ideal level Mies might have been difficult
for other architects to follow: fortunately, at one
simple level of emulation, the clear architectonic
articulation of structure, and structure to skin and
partition, and partition to door-frame and so on, in
Mies' own built work is so clear and develops so
consistently that it has been possible for others to
follow who are prepared to work at it with the same
zeal as Lord Burlington.

26 July 1977, PS.

In keeping with Mies' character and his life-long
work method, there was nothing socially revelatory
or innovative about the Weissenhofsiedlung – it
was the same old villas and apartments and terrace houses. That way the thrust of style itself
could be felt.

'On Innovation'.
Unpublished.

Undated realisation,
late 1970s? AS.

The small man we met at Mies' apartment in the 1950s was probably Eduard Ludwig Primus, killed in a Porsche crash in the 1960s, who taught Stefan Wewerka (see Appendix 2, page 68) when Stefan was 18: very intelligent, direct-line Mies inheritor. Mies introduced him as 'My first assistant' … and they both laughed.

Wewerka, Meeting
in Mies' apartment.
Unpublished.

1983, PS.

Mies used in a rough and ready way the rectangle 'On Krefeld',
plan form and repetition of bays – which devices, published in <u>The</u>
we are now able to see, were the principle formal <u>1930s</u>, Tecta, with
characteristics of the thirties architecture, seen in Alexander Verlage,
the Factory for the Silk Industry in Krefeld,[41] 1933. Berlin, 1985.

1980, November
1984, January 1985,
PS.

The emigration of Mies van der Rohe to the United The 1930s, Tecta,
States in 1938 allowed his thirties to continue. with Alexander
Mies' work and presence in Chicago in the early Verlage, Berlin,
forties passed on to native Americans the radical 1985.
stance of the European designers.

The war seemed to give an obligation to perform
in the post-war period what the architects of the
thirties had promised … in 1945, when it could be
visited again, Prouvé's market at Clichy was six
years old; Mies' earliest IIT building two or three –
or they were just under construction – either way
they were just coming up on our horizon.

And we feel we have a natural right, both as
apprentices-by-proxy and as being members of the
family who 'design-by-thinking-of-the-making', to
inherit as a landscape of the mind the thoughts
and the ways of putting things together of Mies van
der Rohe.

Farnsworth House,
September 1984,
PS.

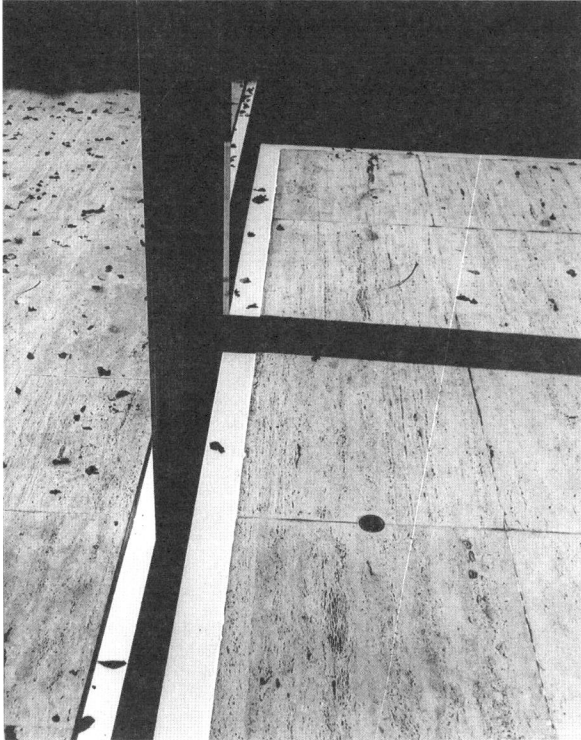

Columns[42] on the platform squarish so one can swing around them and back as small boys do on the lower level of piers.

I want to know more about Lily Reich.°

Re-screening the four colour slides I took on my first visit to Farnsworth House in 1958.[43] The house then was lived in carelessly; that is, without affection between occupier and dwelling. This had depreciated the spirit of the fabric. When a building is in complete dereliction or ruin, and only the air, the trees, the animals and the birds live there, its spirit recovers.

'Going Back,
Workpoints',
Quaderns,
October/November/
December 1984.

° Photograph of
Mies and Lily Reich
in 1933, published in
Ludwig Glaser,
Furniture and
Furniture Drawings,
Museum of Modern
Art, New York, 1977.

IIT Campus,
September 1984,
PS.

44

Everything in Mies was there in Chicago along the tracks, 1958 [PS's first visit to Chicago; second visit 1972].

When IIT is most austere it lends itself best to the ordinary.[44, 45] The credibility of modern architecture as a continuing language was established, for this continent, here.

'Going Back, Workpoints', published in Quaderns, October/November/ December 1984.

45

46

47

48

49

50

30 October 1984,
AS.

'Territory of the
Pavilion', extracts
from a lecture.
Unpublished.

A short stay in the Farnsworth house[46] started me thinking about the <u>state of play</u> of the idyll, the pavilion in its territory. This idyllic possibility was reintroduced into architecture by the Barcelona Pavilion.[47]

The Farnsworth House at Plano, Illinois, the Eames House and Studio in Santa Monica, California, and the Solar Pavilion (the Folly) at Fonthill, Wiltshire, all seem to be offering possibilities for new kinds of light-touch inhabitation. These three pavilions enjoy certain commonalities.

They all accept the sun; the Farnsworth and the Eames control the amount of acceptance by means of curtains and so on.

All have a stable surface immediately outside onto which the pattern of inhabitation can readily be extended.

All take position in their territory so that it becomes the <u>right inhabitation field</u> … most obvious perhaps in the Solar Pavilion at Fonthill in its compound as New Brutalist grandchild of the Barcelona Pavilion.

Inside each pavilion – as indeed within the territory – the spaces can be more or less empty of things, or they can accept a collection of things that are the natural extensions – tentacles if you like – of the lifestyle being created by the inhabitants.

The spaces can be used in a number of ways.

The spaces do not feel empty when departed from, are possessed by a single person; a number of occupants can find a sense of private territory, say on a wet day.

Inside the territory the eye looks down on the stable surfaces or the grass immediately outside,[48-50] looks through the glass at the foreground trees, looks at the middle ground, looks towards the territory's fringe trees … that is, the eye has a sense of possession of a particular aspect of nature in each field of vision, all within the territory.

There is also a sense that the territory beyond is unobtrusively <u>possessed</u>, both visually and as

51

52

53

54

55

56

necessary adjunct, idyll support ... in the Farnsworth, the Fox River, the nature reserve views of the other bank; in the Eames,[51] the Pacific Ocean; the Solar Pavilion, 360 degrees of a Wiltshire horizon comprising one third Fonthill Woods, one third farm land, one third downland.[52]

The seasons can be appreciated – we watch the snow falling in twentieth-century comfort[53, 54] which allows a new kind of awareness of the moods of the time of day or the seasonal weather; the sense of modern man in nature is achieved.[55, 56]

Due to the discretion of the three pavilions, birds, animals, come directly up against them – this interface is supported by part of the territory seeming to be 'as found'.°

The pleasures of occupant as observer are extended into the night since outside lights can continue to offer the territory and allow it to be seen in different ways.

The territories have a sense of vertical depth: in the Farnsworth, the water level then the riverbed of the Fox; in the Eames, the drop from its ledge to the beach and the ocean (as well as the protective height of the bluff above); the Solar Pavilion in its 125-foot-deep well (the same dimension as the length of the compound).

In two of the pavilions their first owners had to leave because their sense of territory became destroyed by noise; the topography of their ledge protects the Eames' territory although the noise level on the coast road below, indeed on the beach, must have at least doubled since the 1950s. It would seem the idyll of the pavilion in the territory is extremely hard to maintain in the car-owning democracies. The desire to get into the country – in the USA to camp, in Europe through the occupation of erstwhile remote properties by weekenders from the 1950s to the 1970s – has moved on in the 1980s to the exit from the cities of the technological cowboys who treat the country as ruburbia.

° Not a characteristic of the Barcelona Pavilion.

57

December 1985, AS.

58

59

60

61

The first impression upon entering the Barcelona Pavilion while under reconstruction[58] is that it is all one-third larger than the pavilion-image that the photographs formed in one's mind. That the majority of these photographs are <u>doctored</u> – their backgrounds' whited-out – has possibly contributed to this loss of scale in the image of the myth.

In the reconstruction, this apparent increase in scale, the travertine expanse[59, 60] – formally accepted as descendant of the Germanic neo-classical tradition[57] – becomes, because of its colour, some sort of <u>desert</u>; which I connect to the idyll of Saint Jerome's restorative 'place apart'. The Mies Pavilion offers the possibilities: in the open, of Saint Jerome in the desert; under cover, of Saint Jerome in his study. For one can add to those instinctive reasons for accepting the Barcelona Pavilion as <u>myth</u>, an inheritance, by osmosis, of this western <u>idyll</u>.

The old photographs of the Barcelona Pavilion were, naturally enough, black and white, but so were all the photographs of our youth. Our generation was in no doubt as to the nature of the materials – (green) marbles, or (golden) onyx.[61] In fact, directed by the photographs, our myth-image is nearer to what they were than the reconstruction

'Mies' Barcelona Pavilion, Myth and Reality', extracts from a lecture, Barcelona, 1986. Unpublished.

is. Yet, because mythical qualities are of their nature somewhat vapourous – and deliberately kept so, that they might continue to inhabit the peaks of one's mental landscape – the information gained from captions to the black-and-white photographs was not so detailed for us to know that two sources were used for the green marbles: Aosta, Italy; and Larissa, Greece.

Marble always engages our consideration because of its surprising composite quality working with the variations of stresses in the depth of its make-up. The pellucid greens; the unforseen portions of apple green; the semi-lucent darkness that requires study to be sure it is still green; an under-sea or much wetter green. Yet in considering these reconstructed qualities – as Mies might have stared into their composition – part of our consciousness is always aware it is not the same marble as made the myth.

What could not be appreciated before the coloured reality was the forest connection.° I find in the Mies building the travertine-contained space becomes a sunlit clearing, the green marbles perform as the forest frame, while the shaft of light beamed down from the slot[62] falls into its new role as a signal of forest and the light-barred metal frames act under their top cover as if they were birch saplings.

There is no doubt in my mind that Mies' Customs House neo-classical and forest experience happened in St Petersburg°° – and I do not mean Mies used literal transpositions, but grasped and turned over something that was indicating to the receptive how to extend the language of an architecture that had to be changed. It is this illusive nature of the invention that is most vulnerable when it comes to myth-reconstruction: the exact touch of the period; the real smell of the period; the impact of minds and hearts; cannot be reconstructed.

The change of mind the original effected cannot be recreated. The building happened when our architectural grandfathers were relatively young; at

° See 'The Grown and the Built', Spazio e Societá 25, March, 1984.

°° See also 'Observation at Makasar Summer Palace, outside Bukhara, Uzbekistan', page 60.

the reconstruction our children, the fourth generation, are on the threshold of middle age.

Experiences of coming face to face with the reality of <u>myth</u> – that is anything that changed our minds in some way simply by our seeing a drawing or photograph and then meeting face to face – are ever-present possibilities. We are used, for example, to meeting a ruin, such as the Parthenon. What is more unusual is meeting the myth that has been lived in: such was the experience in visiting Le Corbusier's apartment ... still outside the door, the myth-image formed by the photographs from the <u>Oeuvre Complet</u> was pure in mind. Once I stepped through the portal, an instant aging – the pristine marble table had been used for thirty years. Consequently, I now carry two myth-images in my mind of the same apartment.

During reconstruction of the Barcelona Pavilion, my eyes having been conditioned by the photographs, the enclosed tank of water[63] called for its surfaces to be made black ... is its progenitor the Lanwehrkanal, Berlin?

The long travertine bench we supposed generated by von Klenze's tufa bench in the Konigsplatz,[64] Munich.°

Our generation cannot think in terms of literal connections; probably that was <u>the</u> lesson from the Heroic Period.

Mies as a choirboy in the Dom, Aachen, probably saw a shaft of light falling into the Romanesque <u>grove</u>; possibly also gained affection for onyx there. Through being a boy in the mason's yard of his father and uncle, he could probably recognise the quality of a block of marble in its raw state. Real experience, observations, the considerations of the inventive mind.

The Barcelona Pavilion stood for difference that risked the neck. The achievement of its happening, that its fabrication became a milestone in many minds.

The myth is of that leap from the Silk Exhibition, from the Otterlo mock-up, into the minds of generations.

° Having used that bench, 1982–83, and Platz a number of times, the relationship was more obvious that simply that of a <u>signpost</u> and the <u>jump</u> Mies made the more exciting because of this. In Munich they say that the space between the Glyptotek, the Pinacothek and the Propylaea was originally not paved and the paving is from the Nazi period. The assumption of this sentence of text is that the tufa bench is by von Klenze.

11 February 1986,
PS.

Mies never failed to 'make a space'. His buildings evolved, from the Afrikanischerstrasse[20–22] onwards, so as to create a territory to themselves: a territory somehow set-apart – as a village church's space is set apart yet gives itself to the community: Afrikanischerstrasse 1926–27; Barcelona Pavilion 1928–29; Seagram Building 1954–58; Dominion Centre 1963–69.[65]

65

'Reflections on seeing an air-view showing Mies van der Rohe's Dominion Centre, Toronto, in an in-flight magazine, London-Barcelona'.
Unpublished.

April 1986, PS.

But for a later generation, familiar through re-pub-
lication with all that travertine in Nazi architecture
and who have been born since Europe has been
colonised by Hilton International, can the Pavilion
be mythical to them? Re-built as a facsimile, can
it still carry the smell of its revolutionary intent?

'All that Travertine'.
Unpublished.

December 1986, PS.

Concerning the Barcelona Pavilion[66] and the <u>way</u>, the <u>predictable promenade</u>.

There is weight to exclude as well as create territory.

The visitor never gets lost.

The visitor can see out.

There is a sense of protection.

'Barcelona Pavilion', extracted from 'More about Conglomerate Ordering', <u>ILA & UD Year Book</u>, 1986—87, integrated in <u>Italian Thoughts</u>, Sweden, 1993.

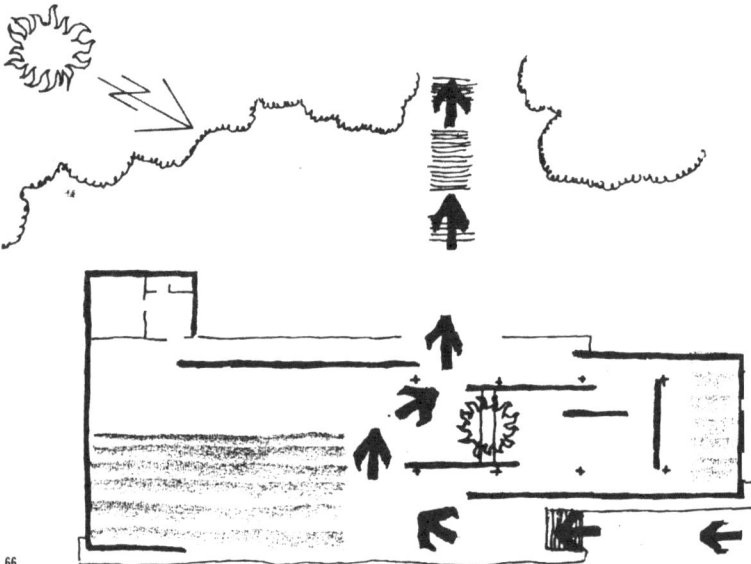

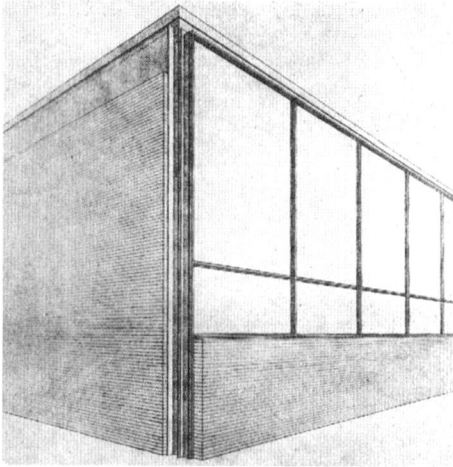

67

December 1985 and
April/May 1986, AS.

'Mies' Barcelona
Pavilion: Myth and
Reality', paper given
at Aachen, 6, 7 June
1986. Unpublished.

Myths probably seed in us at an impressionable age; at a time when we want to be changed.

I concentrate here on reception of myth and response to myth and to reality

As I know nothing of Mies' teaching – beyond one visit to the School in Chicago – I represent the students in Europe taught by the myth of the Barcelona Pavilion. So I will risk a history of myself around the time my mind was seeded by the myth and in this way, not only acknowledge a debt but also try to make tangible the energy of a myth.

I do not know when or what book – or possibly advertisements in architectural magazines – made me accept the Barcelona Pavilion as a myth of purity that belonged to the realm of temples ... possibly it was its rectangularity that made this connection; possibly the unknown material of travertine. Something of this reverence was felt by all, for the Barcelona Pavilion was not cribbed by students in the 1940s for dockers' cafés, artists' studios, or yacht clubs.°

The Mies myth – as all others, ancient and modern – came to me on paper. The myth was as old as myself, taking 16 years to reach me. Modern architecture was still a relatively private matter. I never heard it mentioned that Kurt Schwitters lived the end of his life in the English Lake District.°° I saw his English work around the walls of Mies' Chicago dining room.°°°

When I was in fifth year at Newcastle, PS was at the Royal Academy Schools in London. He wrote that he had discovered Mies in Johnson's book. I received The Architects' Journal on a student subscription and in this had been the first publications of the Mies work at IIT – I sent the tear sheets of the two articles as I did not value them. I may not, at first sight, have realised the same man made the Barcelona Pavilion and IIT. The first full-page illustration was a close-up perspective of part of a corner; quite incomprehensible why anyone should draw large, a rolled steel beam and stanchion and some brick-joints.[67]

I still cannot face brickwork. On Tyneside I was

° PS: One student in my second year, Derek Cole, discovered columns as crosses and separated-out walls, which he presented in dense poster colour. He was not accepted back into the school after return from war service.

°° Eighty miles from Tyneside where I lived.

°°° A phenomenon which supports a point which PS will make, about the time-lag before a myth communicates.

68

surrounded with brickwork still being dirtied by industry.

Bare steel sections for me had been the derelict shipyards of the 1930s; were the gantries of the shipyards; rivetted or welded, they were the skeletons of the ships. The finished object was the cased ship, product of the draughting loft that I used to get taken into, where on the huge tables were the giant, thin boxwood french curves used to draw the ship's profiles, understandably in the same tradition of decision-making as the echinus of the Doric capital.

I had assumed – it proved correctly, when the actual working drawings were exhibited in London in the 1970s – that the Barcelona Pavilion had been – like most Heroic Period buildings – built with the same turn-of-the-century building construction methods which we were taught. So was Krefeld; that we looked at in 1955, returning from La Sarraz.

The work in America is as it looks, an attitude towards technology rather than building construction.

The myth, 'Barcelona Pavilion', was clear in my mind between 1944 and 1948 as an isolate.

That it was an especial kind of myth and not only so to our generation is supported by its Egyptian Isis side that throughout our working life has produced rumours of 'the crates being found'. Mies assured us the stones went back to Germany and were made into fireplaces.

Thirty-seven years came between the myth and the reality of Barcelona Pavilion rebuilt. Thirty-five years of visiting Greek and Roman sites had maintained in my mind the rectangular base of the pavilion as podium;[59] in reality, it reads as dado: domestic rather than isolative or heroic.

My myth of the Barcelona Pavilion is unfurnished, therefore I was attracted by what seemed to be furniture by Giocometti.[68] Perhaps I noticed because 'Signs of Occupancy' is one of our themes.

Most people I have questioned have, like

myself, read the narrow rectangle on the plan of the myth as a cupboard: this assumption was not unreasonable; but it is a translucent light slot.[60] If the visitor entered down-slope, he was welcomed by translucence. You were not, as it were, posted into a dark slot. Surprising is the uncharacteristic segmental arch over the slot, yet in a <u>forest</u> context these light-barred metal frames act as branches above.

The axis of inspection of the pavilion crosses the picture plane; the single axis of penetration into the pavilion makes it in reality a propylaeum. In the myth, the power of the walls running lengthwise of the rectangle obscures its propylaeum nature.

The myth assumes the traditional <u>pavilion as idyll</u> ... the reality is a propalaeum that directs you, turns you through right angles, right or left; a propylaeum to the future in that it is no longer a passive gateway of a single function. You cannot just pass through. The idea is enriched, you are made to experience, consider.

The Barcelona Pavilion rebuilt is strangely de-personalised. Compared with Alfeld, seemingly: 'look, no hands'. Its rebuilding, from roof-on stage to glass-in stage, shows a more permanent structure.[58-62]

I suspect the rebuilt myth will compound an inability to discern between being energised by a myth to make a new language and merely ripping something off without so much as raising a hand in thanks.

Looking back ... in some way we stand with Krefeld, in that we are Europeans with a European morality towards invention. Aware that we are becoming a world of long-arm watchers, watching re-enactments; already inheritors of a couple of generations of re-enactment, for beginning in the 1930s, everything was used by Hollywood; advertising followed; television extends this simulation so that even reporting where the explosion rocks the camera is so edited as to be made equal with entertainment: 'They took us to' is a phrase one can hear from the elderly to whom the television's transportation to an event, a country, is still magic.

But the Barcelona Pavilion stood for difference; its fabrication became not only a milestone in many minds but risk materialised, personified, that was, by its removal, elevated into a myth of classical power.

January to June
1986, PS.

'Mies' Barcelona
Pavilion: Myth and
Reality: the Level of
the Ground',
contribution to Mies
seminar, Aachen,
6, 7 June 1986.
Unpublished.

69

Some six or seven years ago, I picked up a book
from someone else's shelves and read at great
speed an essay which described the steps in the
canonisation of the Barcelona Pavilion.

It said that at the time of its building the pavilion was received coldly or antagonistically, even by
critics who reviewed it from within the Modern
Movement: critics such as – from memory – José
Luis Sert and Alfred Roth.

A re-reading this year of Hugh Thomas' book on
the Spanish Civil War brought one small further
fact which perhaps bears on this rejection.° The
exhibition was made at the time of the right-wing
dictatorship of General Primo de Rivera in Spain;
a period of dictatorship which lasted from 1923
until January 1930.[69] The architects of the second
generation of the Modern Movement were from
just those liberal and professional middle-classes
and would, somewhat naturally, regard any participation in the exhibition as a betrayal … even the
participation of the new German Republic. For
those committed to the left any participation at all
would be immoral.

The pavilion reached me as a real historical fact
through Philip Johnson's book on Mies, published
in 1947, which I bought in 1949. The plan in that
book[70] (there were never any sections of the
Barcelona Pavilion published) reinforced in my
head the myth that the building was essentially a
platform, raised-up clear of the natural ground on
all sides. But Quaderns°° published the original
plan variants and an old photograph from the back
of the pavilion.

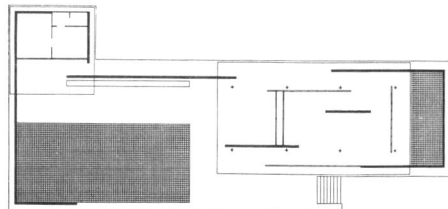

70

° Hugh Thomas, The
Spanish Civil War,
pp 16, 17.

°° The Catalan
architects'
magazine,
October/November/
December 1984.

71

72

In the photograph[71] the back entrance can be seen as being level with the natural ground. Indeed from that side the pavilion was seen down-slope onto the roof.[72] For my myth it was necessary for the pavilion to be demolished after the exhibition closed, thus allowing the idea of the still, perfected, object floating above the ground to become absolute. But now we see it in facsimile, re-built on its old site; and it was not a platform, it was a ledge, a passing-through-stop on a route, more of a propylaeum than a pavilion.

7 June and 7 July
1986, PS.

Listening to Franz Fueg in Aachen,° we realised that Mies' 1930s drawings of Court Houses taught us how to see his sort of space. Space never bleeds out except under control; that is, his buildings, walls, bushes and so on, protect his territory, the territory of Mies' vision of space. The eye never escapes to villas or sheds or parked cars which might overturn the space. The devices which build up Miesian spatial territory mediate between the person and the general. That mediators are necessary, that protection is necessary, is something quite outside the ethos of the twenties, especially of de Stijl, when, as it were, it would be good if every thing was open to every person.

Mies sets up in his thirties Court House drawings architectural space in which some things are open to some persons.

It can be said that we always need protection – a protection different for every tribe in every time. There is now in Western Europe a pressing need for protection from a glut of noise, movement, things … we need to protect our territory more urgently and very differently than Mies can have imagined in the thirties.

This perhaps explains the instinctive move in the 1970s to explore an architectural language of layers and lattices.[73] The drawings made then were made to teach us to see a differently protected territory.

'Thoughts on Protection' and 'Mies van der Rohe: Thoughts after a visit to Aachen'. Both unpublished.

73

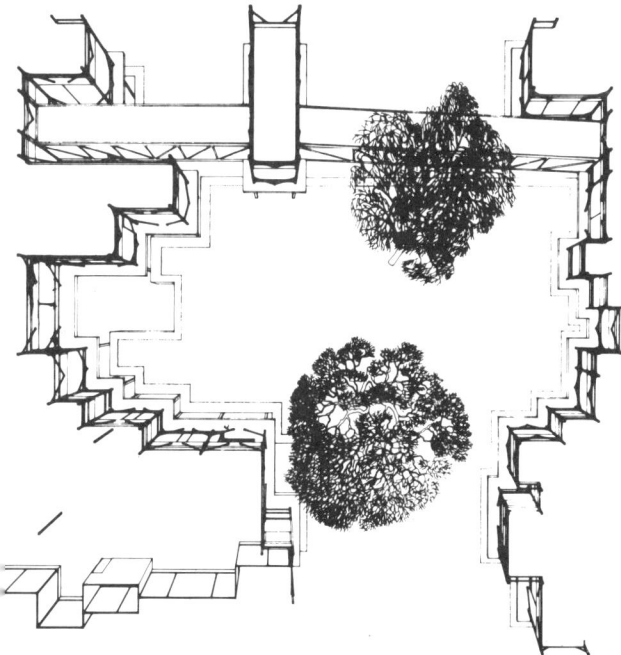

° Although cut short by Christian Norburg-Shultz, the convenor, Fueg's insights were those of a lifetime.

6, 7 June 1986, AS.

Barcelona Pavilion, being a propylaeum,[71, 72] is separate from the pavilion idea.

The Barcelona 'non-pavilion' leads to <u>territory in view</u>, under control, as in courtyard houses; true pavilion – Farnsworth – leads to <u>domain</u>.

Calling Barcelona a 'pavilion' is a misnomer only in so far as it misleads us. It is just that every building in any exhibition is called pavilion. Exhibition buildings are not all pavilions in the sense of a retreat in a park; whereas Thomas Jefferson's Monticello is,[74, 75] in that it rides over its territory and controls it, so that the territory becomes its domain … a true pavilion in the grand manner in that it is 'a restorative place in nature'.

After a certain date – 1955? – Mies turned to the true pavilion and whenever he was asked to do that which should be a low building, Mies used the pavilion form. Congress Hall? – he simply made a bigger pavilion.

'Thoughts on Pavilions'. Unpublished.

76

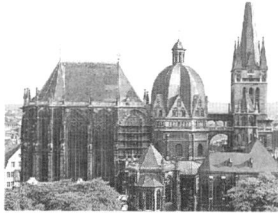

77

78

79

6, 7 June 1986, AS.

'Lessons of Mies Exhibition + Aachen Itself'. Unpublished.

The first building Mies worked on as draughtsman was a department store, now gone, in Flemish style: three equal gables, one central and two pavilion, over large department-store windows. This experience, in a town with a surprising proportion of traditional Flemish town houses,[76] may have caused him to read the whole of Aachen in reverse: that is, as glass held in structurally minimal façades – a structural minimalism.° Mies comes from one of the glassiest parts of Europe: glassiness really built – like Antwerp – stone mullions, transoms.

The Dom school[77] Mies attended for a short period,°° was not only almost under the lantern-like choir, but perhaps more importantly, directly opposite the playground gates is a Wilhelmine gothic revival building – of a quality not unlike a Glasgow building – whose coarse, thin, black, hard, stone columns rise from base to capital through the full height of ground plus two floors.

Aachen was bombed or shelled during the 1939—45 war but sufficient of the remaining houses have the Flemish or Low Countries style of neat, eroded pink brickwork in stone frames, oval windows as a random inset over door or onto stair[78] – unGermanic compared to the monument to Rosa Luxemburg or the Krefeld houses but possibly accounting for Mies' affection for brickwork.

At the Mies/Maillard mason's yard, a machine, once hand-operated, now rebedded and electrified: the present owner claimed Mies had turned the wheel as a child. One is therefore able to postulate that Mies knew all about the likely sizes marble could be obtained in, its thicknesses; the quality of the types of marble/granite; the working of stone, its properties/names/provenance – all related to the luxurious sheet marble used in the Dom: verde antico and purple porphyry. The latter may have given Mies a liking for purple brickwork and open-book marble.

The Eisenbrunnen colonnade of Schinkel,[79] °°° Mies apparently passed every day on his way to the Dom school; something of repetition must

° That would be further absorbed from Amsterdam houses while under the direct influence of H P Berlage (1859–1934) during Mies' year in The Hague, 1912.

°° Common in those days of children finishing school at 12.

°°° Der Mineral-Trink Brunnen auf dem Friedrich Wilhelms Platz zu Aachen, 1823–24.

have impressed itself. The gardens behind may even have had Schinkel cast-iron chairs that would influence the Tugendhat chair.

8 June 1986, PS.

In Aachen, in the Dom, looking at the throne of Charlemagne,[80] it was immediately obvious that the amplitude and the actual physical dimensioning was that used by Mies van der Rohe for the Barcelona, the Tugendhat, chairs. Mies has himself said the Barcelona chair was made for a king.

'Charlemagne's Chair, the Dom, Aachen'. Unpublished.

Checking this observation in the Tecta factory in Lauenforde against the dimensions taken by Axel Bruchhauser of the throne; the interior width is 73 cm which compares with the width of the Barcelona at 75 cm, Tugendhat at 72 cm.

Furthermore, the side pieces of Charlemagne's throne – which give its occupier his hieratic posture – relate directly to the curved side tubes of the earlier Mies chairs[81] which are notorious for the constriction they place on the act of entry and exit from them. They require steps backwards to get in, steps forwards to get out.

Charlemagne's chair as a mini-territory within the Dom.

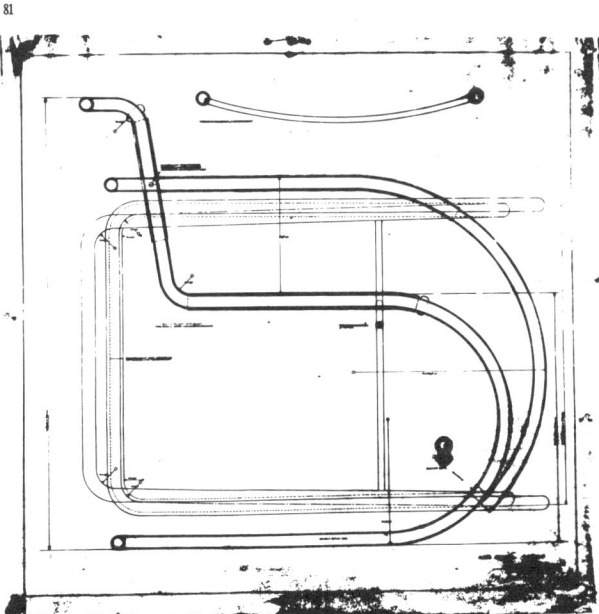

21 June 1986, PS.

A quiet sense of quality is the response to glut in a freely unhistorical, just society.

'Mies Note'.
Unpublished.

16 July 1986, AS.

In 1920 Russian emigrées turned up in Berlin wearing cream silk shirts and matching knitted silk ties: was this when Mies adopted this style, or, like Bismark, was he transformed by the style of Russia while visiting Saint Petersburg?

'Clothes, Berlin, 1920'. Unpublished.

Ely, 20 July 1986,
AS.

Both of us grew up in areas of the north-east of 'The Mind's Eye'. England where there were, attached to the older Unpublished. farmhouses, gin mills of the 1780s agricultural revolution. You might say the 'knocked off corners' aesthetic of the Economist Building – not to say the earlier bold geometry of Coventry Cathedral – owe a debt to these low, hexagonal, half-open buildings with their conical, pantiled roofs.

Therefore it is quite feasible to surmise that Aachen's regional Flemish vernacular should form the mind's-eye of Mies van der Rohe, preparing for his move towards a more equable apportioning of glass to structure.

25 July 1986, AS.

When Mies arrived in Berlin, 1906, the Teitz all-glass façade was ten years old.[82] He may already have seen illustrations, possibly when he was working for the first time as draughtsman on the Flemish-style department store for Aachen. I think the glass proposals of 1920 and 1921, as well as the concrete office block of 1922 (because of its proportions) owe much to the Tietz Department Store.

On seeing Rauch books, in Heinz Rauch Haus, Wuppertal: Mies and Tietz Department Store, Berlin.

Mies must have seen.

Rauch: book: observation. July, 1986

82

curved top balustrade cornice

transparent sloping bar only: big Berlin lamps

tall: incredibly thin.

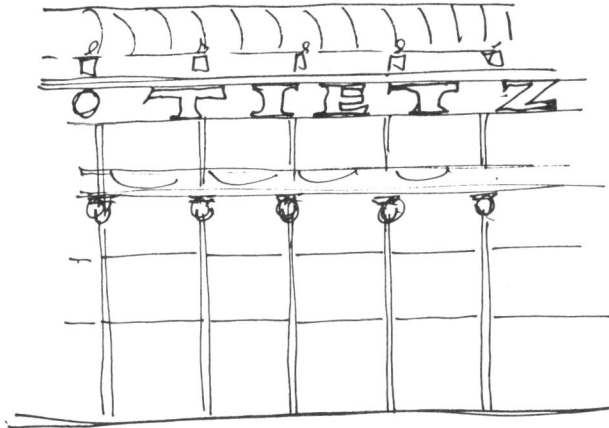

N¹ᴱ Baren, Stuttgart
Tietz warehouse, Berlin. 1896. Leipzigerstrasse.

22 April 1987, PS.

Amost without exception Mies' buildings seem to have the space around within them already. Of course they are cunningly sited and their parts sized to place, but that projection of a field of space around them is more than that.

'The Space Around already Within', on seeing Peter Carter's building, Swindon.

Munich, 5 April
1987, PS.

The best of fifties architecture – such as the <u>green</u> steel and concrete student union building behind the Glypotek in Munich – has the certainty of deep discoveries: those that had been consolidated by Mies van der Rohe at IIT in the forties.

'Consolidation of Mies' Discoveries'. Unpublished.

3, 29 August 1988,
AS + PS.

Mies van der Rohe was in the Netherlands during 1911 and 1912,° to supervise, as assistant to Peter Behrens, the erection of the full-scale on-site mock-up of the Kröller House at Wassenaar near The Hague and subsequently to make his own design and full-scale on-site mock-up for that same house.

'The Jump'. Unpublished.

All the books about Mies speak of his life-long acknowledgement of the Beurs in Amsterdam by H P Berlage, as one of the buildings which set the direction in which his own work was to run: <u>that building was really built</u>.

None of the books mentions, one never heard Mies speak about, another building by Berlage, the Gemeentemuseum[83] in The Hague. Yet the moment one sets eyes on it, images of Mies' brick houses rush into the head.

Is it possible that this building, which was not even designed when Mies was in the Netherlands, was for him a stylistic source?

The Gemeentemuseum is dated 1919–35. That first date is long before those blunt brick houses that sprang into the mind; the Esters House from 1927–30 in Krefeld, the Lange House from 1928 in Krefeld and the Lemcke House from 1932 in Berlin.

The <u>jump</u> seems most evident between the back buildings of the Gemeentemuseum to the plain brick boxes in Krefeld. It is partly in the detailing, but mostly in the cutting-in of the windows into the

° Astonishingly in this same year Mies served as project manager on Behrens' Saint Petersburg Imperial German Embassy site: see Franz Schulze, <u>Mies van der Rohe, A Critical Biography</u>, University of Chicago Press, 1985, p 58.

walls which give to both museum and Mies a kind of conscious banality.[84, 85]

We can assume that Mies would have always had his eye on Berlage and that the museum design must have been published in Holland (and in Germany also?) for its architect was one of the most famous in Europe.

To pursue this jump we need the date of the first fragment built. Did the design change over the long period 1919 to 1935? Was the jump a back somersault, the younger influencing the older? Was there a source common to both for the blunt eye: that is, might there have been some banality in that first full-scale on-site mock-up of Behrens that Mies also put into his second? Did Berlage see them, or one of them, and recognise an interesting new imprint?

October 1988, AS.

The Summer Palace for the last Shah of the Uzbeks was built by Russian Army Engineers; a single storey of an L shape with one leg ending in a large glass conservatory The proportions of the windows of the conservatory, the extent of the view through them, stopped me in my tracks. Here was a conservatory[86] of the turn-of-the-century type Mies must have seen when they were relatively new in St Petersburg and, with their lunettes of coloured glass, part of the fashion for 'Turkish' kiosks, bazaars, verandas, common to Europe at that time. Here was one of his sources of the single-storey house whose large squarish spaces had two, three, walls of glass windows. It is possible that Holland, the land of agricultural glass houses, persuaded him to try a glass house on the client and the building industry.

'Observation at Makasar Summer Palace, outside Bukhara, Uzbekistan'. Unpublished.

January 1990, PS.

On the occasion of
the reconstruction
of 'Patio and
Pavilion' from the
This Is Tomorrow
Exhibition, 1956, in
The Independent
Group Exhibition,
ICA, London, 1990.

In its plan the Barcelona Pavilion is as enigmatic as the Propylaeum to the Acropolis. It is, because of its unsimple nature, what we have termed a 'conglomerate' building: it is of another order than the pavilion, whose type, throughout Europe, we all recognise in the Chinese Pavilion of the English Landscape Garden.

February, April 1991,
PS.

Maybe one can interpret a certain unregarded aspect of the work of Mies van der Rohe as a survival of an order of the Middle Ages – a working of the Gothic mind – for his buildings seem to charge the space around them, make outdoor territories in embryo.

'Functional to Passage', ILA & UD Year Book, 1991–1992, Urbino.

It is this that his long consideration – the arrangement and re-arrangement – of the spaces between buildings was all about. It was not a visual game and the process did not involve the conscious mind. Maybe for a man from Aachen to have the old discipline lingering in him is not surprising.

That space itself can be the matrix of a conglomerate ordering is a statement about this kind of making.

12 December 1991
and 8 January 1992,
PS.

There was a period, say from 1938 to 1947, when Le Corbusier seems to have lost the line. In this period Mies van der Rohe carried the idea of architecture alone. It is from the work of this period that my generation draw sustenance. Those architects that worked for him, and those others who were cast into devotion to him and affection for him, continue to think about the man and his works … from within.

'The Artful Brick',
review of The
Artless Word: Mies
van der Rohe on The
Building Art, Fritz
Neumeyer, MIT
Press, 1991.

There is a kind of parallel workshop version of the life and works …

'I'll tell you one incident that comes to mind on the campus buildings. I'm not quite sure which it was, whether it was the Chemistry Building or the Metallurgy Building, but those buildings all had eight-inch brick walls on the exterior, finished both sides in brick and I remember one particular load of Hanley brick was not a full eight inches long. So when you laid up the course in English Bond with all the headers in one direction and then the next course with all the stretchers in the other direction, it was impossible to get a wall where both sides would look good. You had to have a full eight-inch brick or the whole thing would be wrong. I think it was Ed Olencki who brought up the problem to Mies and he said, "What are we going to do? The bricks are short, so if I flush it out on one side the other side is indented and that doesn't look so hot." And I remember Mies saying, "We'll split the headers, we'll break the headers and stretch it out a little bit"! Mies said that! After all the studies we had made of brick walls as students and after we were told how important it was not to have vertical joints through the wall. I remember being kind of shattered by all of that. So Mies said, "Sometimes the visual side is more important that the construction side."'

From Impressions of Mies, An Interview on Mies van der Rohe His early Chicago Years 1938–58. The speaker is Joseph Fujikawa, who completed his final year of study at IIT in 1943 and worked with Mies until his death in 1969.

Beauty is the radiance of truth.

87

1991–92, AS.
'Afterthoughts on
Reflections', the
outcome of
questions of the
1950s. Unpublished.

On discovering reflections in Hunstanton,[87] 1953–54, we could better read the photographs of MIT[*] and understand what the Barcelona Pavilion, the Glass Exhibit, 1934, and so on, must have been like or intended to be like.

In 1953 we were to see Krefeld.[°°]

Mies must have been informed by van der Leck, for suddenly (after his Otterlo, the Dutch commission) the plans come apart, walls glide off as if on ice skates – the glass the ice?

Then there is the 'glass-stone'. Is this Mies' variation of the Glasen-kette of Taut and Scharoun? Of all architects perhaps since the Goths Mies knew about stone, in an artisan-like way it was part of him; more and more he went as a monumental mason, dressing with the discretion and air of an undertaker.

[*] Which PS would not to see until 1957.

[°°] Directions given by Sam Stevens who had served with the Friends' Ambulance Service in Germany.

21 January 1992, AS.

'After visit to Riehl House, Babelsberg'. Unpublished.

The Reihl house is tiny, its concrete retaining wall is a gesture towards Hellas that is in scale with the cottage-in-the-woods … which its 'vernacular' pediment lunettes signal Mies' recognition that it is not a villa, unlike those around it.

Its antecedents might be various, or even blasphemous in that it reminds one of the building atop a slope, the Behrens Crematorium of 1906 with its loggia (six pillars), pediment with lunette. The small pedimented box on a small podium had many solutions in Delphi,° although none has pediment and podium in parallel. Pergamon would have been another influential built-on slope,°° and the side loggias of the Great Altar of Zeus Soter in the Berlin Museum present four pillars to the down slope façade.

The house is all carefully attentive to a certain taste of use; presumably to Frau Riehl, to whom the smug primness of the photograph of Mies outside the Pergola – maybe taken by her – seems to address itself and is perhaps the last look of sweet success Mies allowed himself until standing inside 860 (when still under construction?).[88]

° Beaux Arts drawing by Albert Tournaire, 1894.

°° Beaux Arts drawing by Emmanuel Pontremoli, 1895, a name that came down to us in the 1940s.

28 February 1992,
PS.

Observation.
Unpublished.

There is never a north point on a Mies plan.

**Appendix 1
Letter from Peter
Carter to A + PS,
28 May 1969.**

Mies has just finished reading your Berlin Essay …
He found your observations on the neutrality of the
façade and the conclusions which you drew from
this of particular interest.

However, he also said that there was a <u>little con-
struction</u> made when you relate him so strongly to
Schinkel. He said that he was not awake to these
things so early. He also did not seem to agree with
your Crown Hall/Altes Museum observations; nor,
those about the boxers outside the IIT Field House.

He enjoyed your comment about children and
Volkswagens and ended by saying again how interesting he found your essay and asked me to write
to you expressing this.

Appendix 2
Stefan Wewerka,
September 1985.

Mies van der Rohe's cantilever chair with wicker-work seat and armrests designed fifty years ago, is now for the first time in production; the design and manufacture being exactly as Mies' original intention. At the opening of the Tecta pavilion, Lauenförde.

The chairs already on the market, with or without armrests, correspond to that intention only in the eyes of the layman.

In the discussions I have had with the Luckhardts, with Prouvé and with young architects, all found it an offence that not only have the wickerwork ends – so critical to the design – been omitted, but these false versions have been made in a slovenly way.

This, the most beautiful chair monument since the throne of Charlemagne, is now in ordinary mass production! A true victory for the Bauhaus vision of the machine as an extended hand used to produce things for daily use and not only for connection of two materials

As an architect I say: the conception cannot be made more pure.

As a sculptor I say: sculpture cannot create a more elevated space.

As a ponderer I ask: how can I connect this purity with grace, sensuality, economy and day-to-day use?

Towards this question, the pavilion is an offering – a first answer!

Appendix 3
1 August 1986, AS.

Letter to Beate and
John Johansen,
extract.
Unpublished.

Through our connections to our architectural grand-fathers we became witnesses to what they stood for, what they contributed, their personal integrity, and so on, we believe we are able faithfully to read the documents of the period 1916–26 as no other person younger than ourselves will ever be able to … that is, we can appreciate their energy; feel through our veins the things happening in Berlin and Weimar during that creative/destructive period.

Therefore, sensing some years ago (c. 1965) that destructive forces were raising their heads again, my reaction was to start what was then intended as a weather sign to ward off the perni-cious warping of the Modern Movement creation-story; I started to write around historical facts, to make them available, palatable, a fiction of inhab-itants of the period 1916–c. 1926. The document is The Earth of the Modern Movement, for short, 1916 a.s.o. The research and illustration collec-tion in archives in Berlin and London took many years, fitted into gaps in work.

In this way I attempt to fulfil our obligation to the inventive capacity of our grandfathers.

  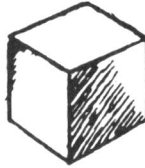  

89

90

91

92

93

In the 1950s the whole design climate was permanently changed by the work of Charles and Ray Eames. By a few chairs and a house.

Now chairs have always been the forward-runners of design change. They have for some mysterious reason the capacity for establishing a new sense of style almost overnight. Rietveld established a whole new design mode with a chair. So did Mackintosh with his.

In the 1940s the Eames moved design away from the machine aesthetic and bicycle technology, on which it had lived since the 1920s, into the world of the cinema-eye and the technology of the production aircraft; from the world of the painters into the world of the layout men.

In a sense both the machine-aesthetic and the Eames-aesthetic are art forms of ordinary life and ordinary objects seen with an eye that sees the ordinary as also magical.°

The machine-aesthetic selected with care those objects from ordinary life that were based on simple geometries[89–91] – on cones, on spheres, on engineers' profiles; objects whose commonality was composable as profiles; that is, pictures could be made from their arrangement and out of which an art-discipline could be erected.°°

The Eames' aesthetic, crystalised in the house at Santa Monica Canyon, California, 1949[92, 93] (as the machine-aesthetic was given canonical form in the 'dwelling unit' in the Pavilion de l'Esprit Nouveau at the Exposition des Arts Decoratif, Paris, 1925), is based on an equally careful selection, but with extra-cultural surprise, rather than harmony of profile, as its criteria. A kind of wide-eyed wonder of seeing the culturally disparate together and so happy with each other. This sounds like whimsy, but the basic vehicle – the steel lattice frame in the case of the house, the colour film and colour processing in the graphics work, the pressings and mouldings in the case of the furniture – are ordinary to the culture.

And this is what separates the Eames' 'selection and juxtaposition' technique from neo-Victo-

Summer 1966, PS.

'Just a Few Chairs and a House: an Essay on the Eames Aesthetic', Architectural Design, September 1966.

° This sounds like a description of the role of Hollywood films as myth-maker to America.

°° See Ozenfant's The Foundation of Modern Art.

94

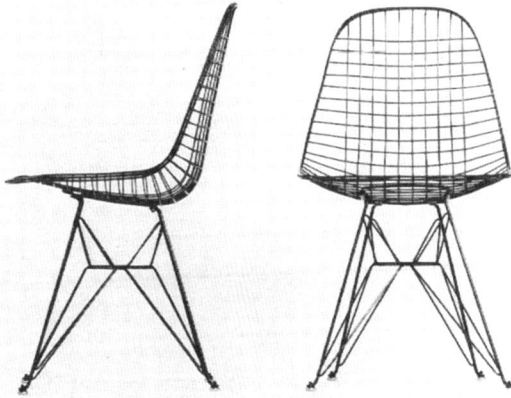

rian screen-making and pop-art forms of either the Barbara Jones° or the Peter Blake°° sorts.

Charles Eames is a natural Californian Man, using his native resources and know-how – of the film-making, the aircraft and the advertising industries – as others drink water; that is, almost without thinking. And it is this combination of expertise and the availability of the expertise of others which produces the apparent casualness that is special to the American life-form and its art-form.°°°

And, as it is the Californian Man's real originality to accept the clean and pretty as normal, it is not surprising that it is the Eames who have made it respectable to like pretty things. This seems extraordinary, but in our old world pretty things are usually equated with social irresponsibility.

95 We can be persuaded to accept the pretty because their work is by no means without a sense of law. When we say 'that's a very Eames photograph' we all know what that means. It is a special way of looking at things, a special sort of composition.[94] It communicates a love of the object photographed, a kind of reverence for the object's integrity. This is what gives their whole output cohesion.

Before Eames, no chairs of the modern canon were in alternative coloured versions, or really light in weight, or not fundamentally rectangular in plan – the chairs of Rietveld, Stam, Breuer, Le Corbusier, Mies, Aalto.

Eames chairs[95, 96] are the first chairs which can be put into any position in an empty room. They look as if they had alighted there – that crow in the wire-chair photograph[97] is no coincidence. The chairs belong to the occupants, not to the building. Mies chairs are especially of the building and not of the occupants. Maybe what worries one about the Eames library-chair-with-footstool, is that it is a reversion to the club chair – immovably part of the club.

The Eames chairs of the new canon are more like the pre-Courrèges clothes of the occupants;[98] pretty, light, non-geometric, apparently casual.

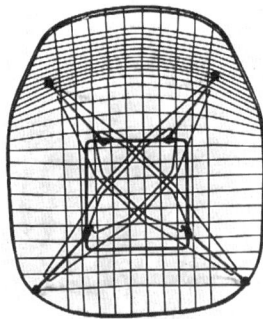

° Black Eyes and Lemonade Exhibition, Whitechapel Art Gallery, London.

°° An English genre painter.

°°° And is presumably why Zen was so popular on the West Coast. Bad Day at Black Rock was of the same period, the mid-1950s.

95

96

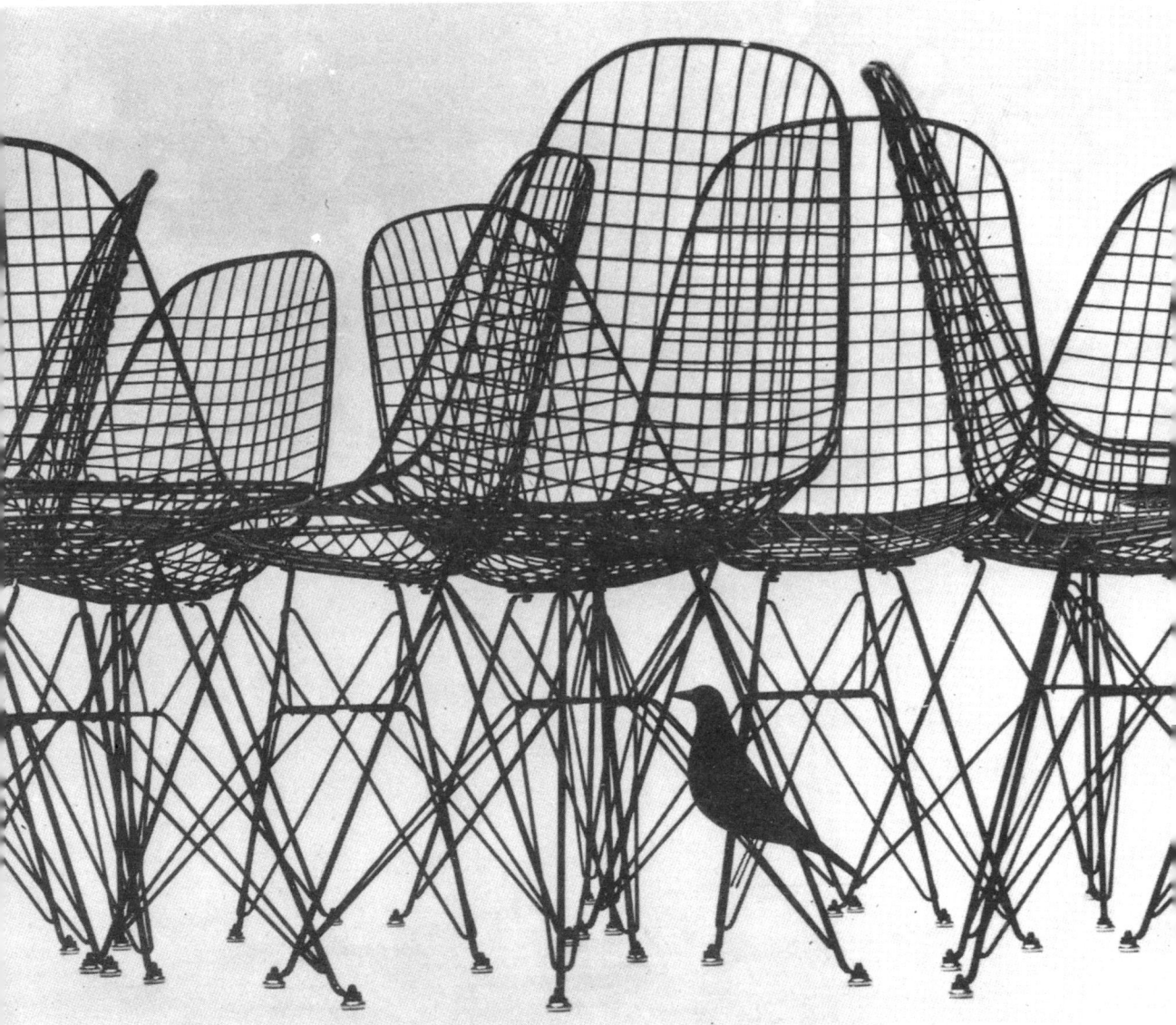

98

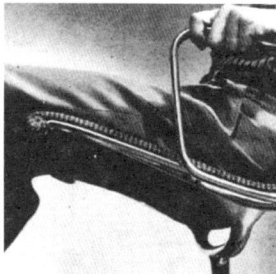

99

100

They use nylon, stretch vinyl, fibreglass-reinforced plastic, all of which can be self-coloured and which carry no overtones of furniture from other cultures. They use aluminium castings and wire struts which remind one, but only if one thinks about it,[99, 100] of new and old aeroplanes respectively, not of other furniture.

A lot of energy has been poured into their detail; it is workmanlike, explicit, even eloquent, but it is quiet. They can be photographed as a fragment, they can be enjoyed as a fragment. They have high object-integrity.

When the Santa Monica House[101] was first published Europeans assumed its look of fragility was a consequence of being able to not worry about the weather problems in an equable climate. But it is stoutly built and equipped to bourgeois standards. Its lightness, its flicker of change, is its style.

By the late 1950s the Eames way of seeing things had, in a sense, become everyone's style.

101

Summer 1966, AS.

I can see the part played by Ray Eames in all that they do: the attention to the last detail of the collected material; the perseverance in finding what exactly is wanted, although the seeker may not actually know the exact object until it is finally seen; the stoic pleasantness that jollies along everyone to the bitter end, for there no doubt that assistants and clients go out of their mind towards the end, if not at stages in between. The principal does, him- or herself, but yet cannot afford to, if the job really has to be done to the perfection imagined.

The prettiness of our lives now I attribute to Ray even more than Charles; we would not be buying flower-patterned ties but for the Eames' card game. It is possible Nigel Henderson° could have led us to the ephemera of life – the penny whistle, the Woolworth's plastic toy or Christmas decoration, the German pressed-metal toy and the walking robots – via photographs of old boots, doors, bits of sacking, but I think it is to Ray and Charles Eames we owe the debt of the extravagance of the new folk purchase: fresh, pretty, colourful ephemera. The Eames allowed us to know Girard and all the cheap Mexicana and candles available to American tourists. The Eames made Girard respectable-pop for Habitat and for Enid Chanel to take the clashing pink colours aboard as house colours.°° The Eames' films gave new life to our inherited toys so that they did not have that peculiar front-parlour-collection chill of Black Eyes and Lemonade.°°°

Our generation were as children reborn from post-war Britain to love objects of a particular international flavour. The Eames gave us courage to make sense of anything that attracted.

In Japan what became suddenly very clear was the Japanese influence in the West Coast, the luxury of the spotlessly clean simple interior, beautiful wrappings, Kleenex. The influence of the West Coast comes to us through the Eames. We still see Eames in films benefiting from the round-the-corner facilities, the developed technology of the film

'Eames: and now Dhamas are dying out in Japan', Architectural Design, September 1966.

° Photographer, 1917–86, sender of ancient postcards magicked over by anotation or collage; see Uppercase 2 + 3.

°° Does the Peter Blake/Joe Tilson generation know the people who made so much of their ephemera acceptable? I think it evaded the generation younger who in the 1960s, 1970s, bought the floral prints, bunches of dried flowers, folk kitchenware, Mexican coloured furniture, and so on, on offer at Conran's Habitat.

°°° Exhibition by Barbara Jones, Whitechapel Art Gallery, 1940s.

102

103

world. Who influenced who out west? Did the Eames influence help create Disneyland or was there another influence creating both these and the historical collection perfection that got into coloured westerns mid-1950s – the right period enamelled coffee can and cup which James Stewart or Burt Lancaster drink out of and so on?

The West Coast world supports the Eames. The Eames support the West Coast world for us and help support our European dream of America as a great free place to be in. In some way they are the other extreme of the Dhama bums who live off the bottom of the West Coast literary world. The Eames are the smiling Dhamas who live in the clouds about Los Angeles.[102] They are our 'Los Angelos' – who providentially provided us with the furniture to put in perspectives of buildings.°

Again, it all comes to us because of the available-round-the-corner technology of America. If you drew a perspective of an interior before Eames' furniture, there was no chair that you could draw in after the Thonet Le Corbusier used, or the first period modern made by Le Corbusier; and none of this could be bought in England in the 1940s and 1950s. The British Thonet to be found in second-hand shops was different from the Paris flea-market Thonet. The reproduction modern phenomena started in the mid-1960s. In the 1950s there was the British Roorkee[103]°° or Bengal camp chair available at the Army and Navy. It was the world of the horrors of the Festival of Britain and so on. The Eames' chair was like a message of hope from another planet.

° I refer to the blackbird and post blackbird era metal-framed chairs. The early period plywood and adjustable shelving, coffee tables, do not speak in any way for us.

°° Roorkee is the junction on the railway to Debra Dun from Delhi via Saharanpur, India.

Winter 1965–66,
PS.

'Concealment and
Display: Meditations
on Braun',
Architectural
Design, July 1966,
and integrated into
Without Rhetoric,
Latimer, 1973.

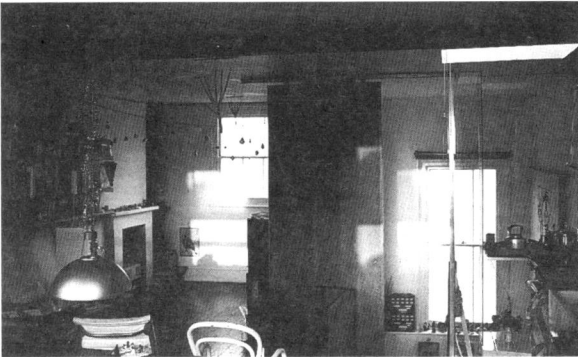

104

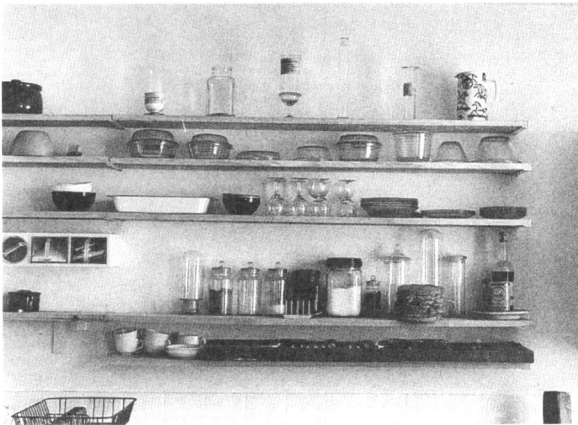

105

Design techniques for pop objects and appliances assume that they will be used where there are no other similar objects: the transistor radio used on the picnic at the road edge or for walking down the street with; the portable dish-washing machine in the appliance-free kitchen with more than enough surfaces to put things down on. In these situations their symbolism can speak and in the early days we welcomed such distinct pronouncements.

But postulate a room full of electronics – say in a ship, or a fully mechanised Swedish kitchen. In these situations, object symbolism is not only unnecessary but can be downright dangerous or unhygienic: the whole assembly has to work together and speak of its use. The armoured leads to the aerials of the ship's radio-room have no need of styling to symbolise power of communication; those plain stainless steel fronts are modern living, not the front-runner or the substitute for it. Pop styling is specific to its situation and moment.

So also is what we have called the 'Eames' Aesthetic' – the 'select and arrange' technique which we have used in the designing and equipping of our own houses and which we still regard as a valid technique for the organisation of relatively simple objects, mechanisms and services in buildings where they can be known about in detail and entrained into the design process.[104, 105] This of course, as a design method, is close to flower arrangement and to good taste in the furnishing of rooms with collector's pieces: it uses things for what they are, each object being enhanced and speaking more clearly of itself by virtue of the arrangement.

But into an arrangement of traditional domestic objects, introduce a new need, say for a family-size washing-up machine: there is no past production to choose from, the machine is large, the product availability will be small and in any one year the styling of one is pretty much like the others. The arrangement cannot normally absorb it: the design method faces collapse.

Winter 1966, PS,
Without Rhetoric,
extracts from
Technische
Universität, Berlin,
paper, March 1966;
Latimer, 1973.

In the Crystal Palace the surface is a regularly seamed glass skin which has no representational function as to structure, or arrangement, or determination of the thing it covers.

The decision on the size of the unit of repetition for a seamed glass skin is similar to any other decision on the unit size of sheet material – with stone facings or glass it is traditionally related to the whole of which the units form part, but with plywood or patent glazing the unit is almost certainly in practice that of the standard economic size of the material.

When a building is made of such standard pieces it would seem that it should be thought about in terms of these pieces, the whole derived from the part in some way – an inversion of the classical tradition. When the skin of a building is glass, or tinted glass, what is inside is pretty explicit anyway. That which is inside can be the carrier of the formal idea in the traditional way, or can become the scaffolding for 'a graphics of occupation' in the Eames' way; that is, part of a kind of visual conversation between the inside volumes, the seamed glass skin and the occupiers' activities.

106

Undated, assumed
to be after 1970,
AS.

The point of examining the Eames phenomenon was because of their shattering of the solid concept of the chair leg; of concept thinking in black and white.[106] This last we are only just breaking down because of the realisation that ordinary people, with colour supplements and colour television, are losing the ability to think – as it were in shorthand – in black and white … and children may never know. Maybe even dreams are coloured now.

The Eames' light-hearted thinking in featherweight climate-bits-and-pieces seeming off-the-peg-architecture … the do-it-yourself out of gorgeous catalogues, the Sears-Roebuck thinking … the whole of the blow-up, plug-in, camp-out, dump-digging type of thinking and living had flown off the spinning Eames like mud off a truck tyre.[107]

Purpose unknown but typescript annotated as to illustrations. Unpublished.

107

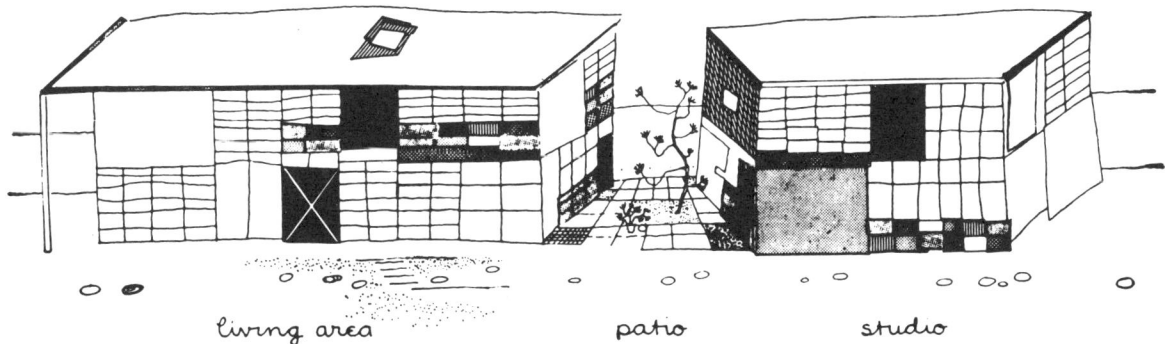

living area   patio   studio

Sheffield, Upper
Lawn, London.
August 1978, PS.

Charles Eames was one of those rare persons who in their work, their sayings and their life, seem to gather up and re-project the whole store of idealism that the Americans have inherited. He was for me the living Jefferson – the very confidence of his life came from his sense of the skill of his fellows and his pleasure in the abundance of the American land.

'Charles Eames,
1907–78', obituary,
RIBA Journal, 10
October 1978.

In the week of Eames' death the fields around me were harvested,[108] as they are every year, by a lean, brown, grey close-cropped, quiet, middle-American. To watch man and machine at work is to sense that in such men there is a circuitry of the brain that no European possesses. They work with a style that is artisan and princely at the same time.

It was the intention of the citizen-philosopher-princes of the earliest years of the Republic that this should be so. Many Americans now live this dream of a useful, proud and quiet individual life: but in some few the ideal becomes conscious, becomes a kind of moral force; to be felt by others, to manifest itself as fresh thoughts and fresh things from a still-new land.

108

Summer 1979, AS.

Two weeks ago, I was in Haifa when I entered an Opening of the explanatory exhibition and immediately my eye Eames exhibition, was drawn to a familiar history-fact-panel on the IDZ, Berlin, 5 wall … fresh, cream-coloured background papers, September 1979, bold white dates of history on a top black strip; extract from a well-chosen, matched images laid on coloured paper delivered on paper – sea green, grey, bronze gold – the pre-the occasion. sentation neat. To me, Haifa was as surprising a place to find myself in as would be, say, Dublin. However, I can imagine a similar Eames-influenced wall display of information might be found, made, in Dublin. People everywhere have been influ-enced, almost without their realising it, by the Eames' non-partisan selection … the Eames' eye for fresh families of things.

To the European eye, the Studio[109] was in a place of no quality, that could have been in the out-skirts of a Greek or an oil-rich place. But its older relations were the film studios, workaday, bland containers where magic was ever freshly made. And it is this continual re-making of freshness and magic that is the Eames' contribution. The anony-mous outside of the film studio was for most peo-ple the secret home of the magic factory.

The home of magic most people know (from pho-tographs) is on a shelf above the Pacific. The Eames entered the consciousness of most archi-tects by re-making and giving magic to the con-tainer called house.

Built in 1949, this house was already nine years old when our first slides were taken.[110] Perhaps because of the climate that drew the film industry to California, the house – in terms of European architectural years – seemed to have hardly aged at all.° Perhaps some growth of plants is obvious between one set of slides and another, perhaps the photographer has become more romantic in 1979, twenty-one years after the first set of pho-tographs, yet the Japanese influence was recog-nised in 1958.

Ray remained in this domain until her death in ° Indeed, at the 1988. It is in the arrangement of possessions that time of Ray's death, we think of Ray's hand. We have learnt to see the 1988, it had not yet been repainted.

pleasure of arrangement, like 'apples on a plate'. We see our own events the Eames' way ... the placement of ordinary things so that they become honourable objects. We have the pleasures of collection as trophies of the chase of the discerning eye.

The Eames' cards gave us the courage to collect whatever pleases us. Hardly anyone has escaped the influence. Ephemera and its consideration, becomes part of an intellectual activity.[111] Any one of the streams of Eames' activities would have been enough of a life: exhibitions, explanatory panels, multiple-screen display of matched slides; the House, the cards; the films; the chairs – even the chairs that do not readily spring to mind when we say 'Eames chairs' – represent an amazing body of work: 1942, 1944, 1945, 1946, 1954, 1956, 1960, 1962, 1963, 1969, 1971.

What we like to call the 'Blackbird wire chairs', emanating from 1948 experiments, the 1950 polyester fibreglass shell and the welded mesh; and the aluminium group of 1958, swivelling, underbow chassis, pvc covered, on star bases; these two peaks have perhaps overshadowed the soft pad group of 1969.

Comparable magic in interiors and chairs was wrought by Margaret Macdonald and Charles Rennie Mackintosh of the proto-Modern Movement: Lily Reich, Charlotte Perriand collaborated with Mies and Le Corbusier of the first generation. However the technological forebears of the Eames can only be American – the Wright brothers. The Eames, mutually creatively supportive, are a Modern Movement phenomenon of its second generation.

111

January 1980, PS

'As the forties and fifties recede we can see that the Eames and Prouvé enlarged the vocabulary and permanently changed the inherited language – for many architects now speak that extended language with fluency'. So I have already said, but of course it is really only 'with various degrees of fluency', for with any extended language, if the new words and formulations are picked out from their inherited supportive base and used in isolation, it can seem as if there has been a reduction of their expressive possibilities, rather than an enlargement.

'Eames: Thoughts Since the Winter of 1978.' Unpublished.

The Eames' invented usages are complex and deeply-rooted. Take for example the Eames 'flat-on' photograph: this way of recording seemed to me to transmute what is photographed to read as a surface-in-itself; a wonderful realisation of a characteristic of colour film and colour printing from film. When I discussed this with Ray Eames, her immediate response was, 'Yes, but the things photographed still exist in their real space.'

It now seems to me that these 'flat-ons', like the much-published child-like line drawings of their own house, hold an illusion of many perspectives, held loosely, as if by weak magnets, onto the picture plane.

And further, that something similar seems to be the Eames' general compositional method. Their own house has in fact many separate concentrations. It is wholly free from ideological obsession with horizontal one-point perspective or with one-point technology ... lightly spot-welded together the as-found industrial frame and windows may be; but where parts of the fabric must unavoidably be touched by the body – for example in the tight space of the spiral stair enclosure – each part is specially made, is comfortingly solid to the touch: nothing would abrade a clumsy elbow. Each item is a separate idea-focus; as it were, a separate perspective.

Untouched by centristic geometries, the Eames stay with the magic of rectangle and repetition that was the gift of the thirties. But within repetition –

the repeated upright kiosks of the Franklin/Jefferson Exhibition, the repeated same-card size of the House of Cards, the gathering strength in repetition of the wire-frame chairs, the repeated rectangular separate frame fragments of many of the films (a mode which is quite distinct from the continuous flowing-image and narrative of feature films), they have performed a transformation of what they inherited.

Through the Eames, in the old artisan way, the tradition of the Modern Movement has been passed on, quite unconsciously in the process of their learning from those who were doing something well ... and from that their invention and power of renewal has flowed.

Let us hope that our successors can feel that we in our turn had the patience and the thoroughness to learn from the Eames.

1980, PS.

In the second generation of the Modern Movement it was through exhibitions that the Eames first extended their inherited language, eventually dispensing with almost all obvious devices from the 1920s and 1930s – freestanding screen walls, tubular frames and so on – the exhibition material becoming itself the means of spatial organisation. The Eames' understanding of the material had the effect of renewing the objects they showed so that they were seen as if for the first time; their qualities were thrown into the space of their setting, fusing with it. This, one feels sure, was also the experience in Le Corbusier's Pavilion de l'Esprit Nouveau with the grey-painted Thonet bentwood chairs, the common water decanter and wine glasses, becoming as if they had been freshly invented.

'Three Generations', ILU&AD Annual Report 1980 (Urbino), and 'Eames: World of Franklin, Jefferson', integrated in Italian Thoughts, Sweden, 1993.

The Eames' travelling exhibition The World of Franklin and Jefferson, made for the bicentenary, in 1975, of the American colonists' rebellion, was a freestanding scatter of screens – rather like up-ended, image-encased brown place-mats – enshrining documents and relics; one open space inhabited by an enormous stuffed buffalo.

Potentially the layout of the exhibit was true to the native American architectural space-notation-by-interval and true also to something special in the Eames themselves, their understanding of the pleasure, the wonder, the many layeredness of the information to be gained from the real. Yet this exhibition passed over some edge of what we were used to being able to find in exhibitions. There was a minusculism, an attention to details to try to communicate the spread of the Franklin/Jefferson inheritance; illustrating their many-faceted lives not found in political histories. The exhibition data made researchers out of the visitors although they belonged to an age used to packaged products, even packaged data. It was a kind of old man's savouring of information, against a background of what was happening to American culture and its over-running everything in its path. Perhaps the buffalo was a handsome

112

reminder of that tendency.

There is a striking coincidence of stance between the immediate post-war exhibitions of the Eames and the staging of the plays of Berthold Brecht: each it would seem felt a 'compulsion towards the real', a desire for the sense of intention to be carried by free-standing 'real' things and by managed light. In Brecht's productions in East Berlin in the 1950s,[112] the observer was transfixed by a remote reality intensified (symbolised by everything being touched by grey); freestanding stage objects and actors more real than real. Indeed the lighting and the setting might have seemed to overwhclm the author's stated intention except in its aim to hurt as it penetrated; to change minds.

Urbino, London, 1980, PS.

When direct communication begins, mutual regard and a sense of a common work allows influence both ways; the elder using and learning and borrowing from the younger – as well as the other way round – across generations who are at work at the same time.

'Three Generations', ILU&AD Annual Report 1980 (Urbino), and The 1930s, Tecta/Alexander Verlage, 1985.

We ourselves are very attentive listeners and watchers of everything that the Eames' have made. We have taken their invention of the 'flat-on colour documentation' of objects as part of the way we now also work.[113]

Eames House,
February 1983, AS.

Information from
Ray during stay in
the house.
Unpublished.

The house, 1945–49: John Entenza thought of buying plateau, shared. Plateau known about for a long time but Will Rogers would never sell. Family sold.

Bridge the first scheme and structure on site when price went up and became worth three times as much therefore thought why be so wasteful? … and a survey of site found trees in a straight line … all plateau impenetrable at time … idea to excavate/cut into cliff behind and see how much space could be built for the same amount of box section steel with zigzag beams: result three times as much space nearly and more reticent idea of building … the bridge a young idea.

Blackbird dates from 1951 wire chair.[114]

114

St Valentine's Day
1984, AS.

The Eames could raise anything to the power of
ten.

'On Eames'.
Unpublished.

November 1984–
January 1985, A+
PS.

So it is in America with the Eames that the period
– the 1930s – closes.
   The Eames' work is hopeful, uncynical, socially
engaged: they are consumers of the available technologies and to them the pure scientist is a figure
of wonder. All these are characteristic of the
designers of the thirties.

The 1930s,
Tecta/Alexander
Verlage, 1985.

1985, PS.

The process of putting together the images and
texts to make the document called <u>The 1930s</u>° led
to something unexpected: that it was in America,
in the late forties and with the native-born Eames°°
that the European thirties ended. The act of arrang-
ing the images in date order had found the Eames
occupying a place in the European generation succession of Modern Architecture.

If one asks who, of the Second Generation in
Europe, captured the essence of his period in furniture, the answer must be Marcel Breuer.°°° When
the Eames were at their start point, Marcel Breuer
was in America. In the same way as when one sees
the drawings of the Beard House°°°° one says, 'the
Eames' House starts here', on sight of a photograph of Breuer's aluminium lounge chair°°°°° one
says: 'the Aluminium Group starts here'; for line
is in the eye of a single generation and fabrication
and process are tied to what is uniquely available
to that generation. The profiled aluminium parallel
side rails with flat steel seat supports between,
the way the yoke is fixed to the side rails in the
Breuer aluminium lounge chair, tell one that somehow, through some channel, these devices,
invented by Breuer for his 1933 chair, hovered in
the air to achieve a further flowering in the minds
of the Eames.

The Eames' aluminium group chairs, as they
evolve – the side rails toeing-in, varying in thick-
ness, like those of a sledge[115] or the shafts of a
cart; the cast aluminium yokes branching to keep
the shafts apart – become something different and
quite new.

The black laced-frame of the wire chair – its two-
part cover indisputably a separate and changeable
set-of-clothes – states the roles of the different
materials so that the separate quality of each
becomes explicit. The explicitness becomes a continuing endeavour of the Third Generation.

In the ten years from 1948 to 1958 the thirties
period-feel becomes the past and the feel of the
fifties is established.

'The Eames Within
their Generation'.
Unpublished.

° <u>The 1930s</u>,
Tecta/Alexander
Verlage, 1985.

°° Charles, born St
Louis, Missouri,
1907; Ray born
Sacramento,
California, 1912.

°°° Marcel Breuer,
born Pecs, Hungary,
1902.

°°°° Beard House,
Richard Neutra,
1934.

°°°°° <u>Marcel Breuer,
Furniture and
Interiors</u>,
Christopher Wilk,
MOMA 1981, says
that the Breuer
winning designs for
the 1933
International
Competition for the
Best Aluminium
Chair (jurors
included Giedeon,
Gropius, Le
Corbusier) had, by
1934, already been
extensively
published in
architectural and
design periodicals.

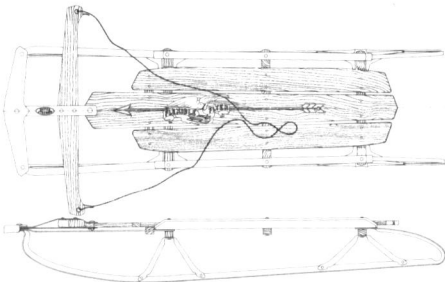

28 February 1988,
PS.

'From Fact to Icon
or Puritanism
Confounded'.
Unpublished.

The Eames' Aluminium Group Furniture, 1958–88, useful everyday for everyman 1958, belonging to the user not the building, sitting like pets, expect to move anytime, moveable with one hand … 1958 die-cast aluminium; 1988?

The wire and plastic chairs are really light: look light, are light. Small feet, thin legs like gazelles/springboks, ready to move, jump at any time.

The Aluminium Group are like the old kitchen chairs, more robust, expecting rough wear, but still to be moveable with one hand whilst the other did something quite different: held a plate, made a point.

1988: shiny with finger marks! Must certainly leave the kitchen, and anyway it asks for attention too strongly for us to be able to make a point whilst trying to move it with one hand – the improved chair is making an insistent point of its own.

Their design stages seem to be two languages in aluminium and one other language of modification.

1988, AS.

'Observation on reading A Field Guide to American Windmills', T Lindsay Baker, University of Oklahoma, Norman, 1985.

116

The assumption that the plywood chairs were more Ray than Charles, because of their Hans Arp styling, in which graphic she made so many of the covers of <u>Californian Arts and Architecture</u> in the late 1940s and early 1950s, has perhaps to be modified in the light of certain American windmills: namely the 'Iron Turbine' windmill,[118] that demonstrated 'that an all metal windmill could do the work of a wooden mill, but also that a metal mill could withstand severe winds and could be repaired without the difficulties that many users expected.'°

During the childhood of the Eames the American landscape would have been dotted with these things, of hundreds of different patented designs. It could be that even the wire chairs owe their confidence and extraordinary jump to these mill structures.[116, 117]

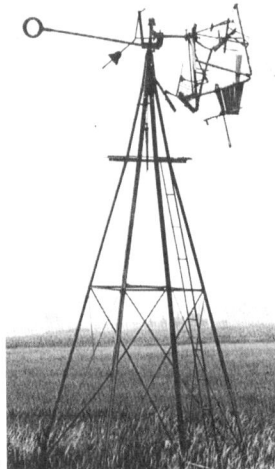

117

° The British tend to link the name of these field windmills to artesian wells.

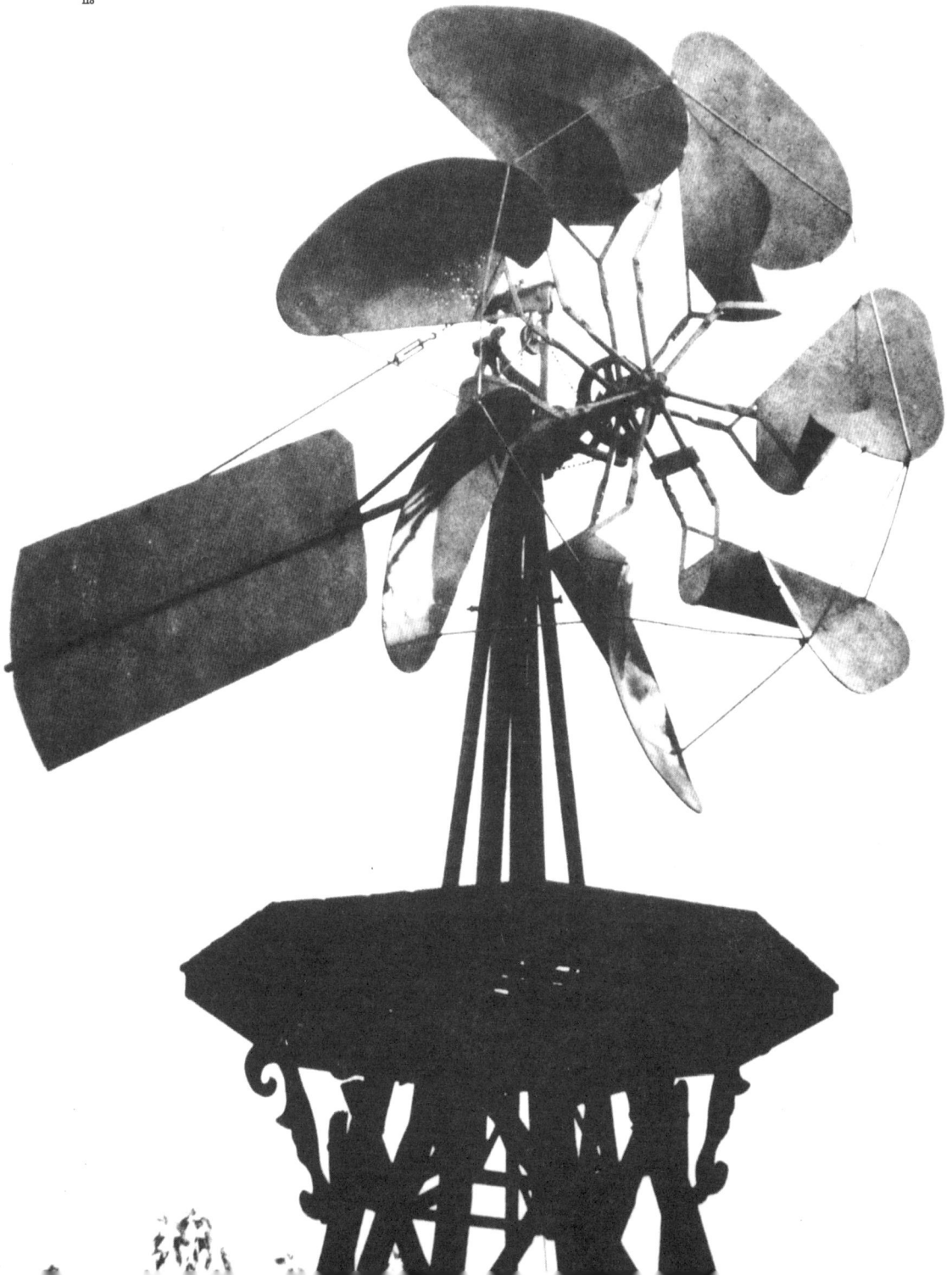

14 October 1988,
PS.

'I must put things in order': Ray Eames … photographs A + PS, large; photographs Λ + PS, small; the note says.

'Putting in Order: on Ray Eames'.

A palimpsest of a January's takings of photographs.

A compost of images: they cannot be put in order … it is painful; Ray had ten years of necessary pain.

When needed, the search makes them live again.

23 April 1988, AS.

119

The Eames' <u>House of Cards</u>[119] was published in 1952. Charles Eames died in 1978. Ray Eames, until her death in 1988, continued working in the studio, 901 Washington Boulevard, Venice, California, sorting their belongings, their archives, their films, variously promised to national collections.

    The Eames' vision was epitomised and packaged in their <u>House of Cards</u>, for, unlike the films,° the cards made available their aesthetic, not only to every one but to every age of person at any time. We used to play Kim's Game;°° asking each other for 'Czechoslovakian glass beads', 'Two red apples on a blue and white plate'. I think the Dreaming Eames would like themselves celebrated this way.

'Eames Dreams, 1988 + 1989'. Unpublished.

° For which you needed a projector until 1991 when the first videotape of a selection of the films became available: all you then needed was a machine that could run American videotapes.

°° Rudyard Kipling's <u>Kim</u>.

7–10 December
1990, PS.

In 1945 – the year the war ended – Charles Eames and Eero Saarinen made their initial proposal for Case Study Houses 8 and 9. In this proposal there was a house and studio for the Eames and a separate house for John Entenza – the sponsor of the Case Study Houses and the editor and owner of the magazine <u>Arts and Architecture</u> in which the proposals were published.

    The site was a real one. Eames and Saarinen wrote of it in the issue of December, 1945: 'This is ground in meadow and hill, protected on all sides from intrusive developments, free of the usual surrounding clutter, safe from urban clatter; not, however, removed from the necessary conveniences and the reassurances of city living.'

    The Eames House at this time sat on the hill at one end and over the meadow at the other on two thin cross-braced supports, with a cantilever beyond, The Eames called it the Bridge House.

    There was a three year interval between the publication of the initial project in December 1945 and the start on site in early 1949.

    In 1947 Mies van der Rohe made an installation of Eames' furniture for the Museum of Modern Art's Exhibition, 'One Hundred Useful Objects of Fine Design'. Certainly it is unlikely that Charles Eames was innocent of the American work of Mies – the Johnson book on Mies was published in September of that same year by that very museum. The book has in it Mies' sketch for a glass house on a hillside, c. 1934 which is the probable base source for the Eames' 1945 Bridge House: the notion would have trickled through to Charles Eames via the architecture culture generally.

    Mies' built work at IIT – which is also in the Johnson book – especially the Minerals and Metals Research Building from 1942–43, with its coolness, its regularity and its standard steel window sashes was something different. It had a quality which somehow opened the gate to another way. A way retreated from, or not regarded, by Mies; but followed by others.

    So, somehow through Mies, through a rejection

'Phenomenon in Parallel: Eames House, Patio and Pavilion', lecture delivered in relation to the exhibition <u>The Independent Group</u> in which the reconstructed Patio and Pavilion travelled London, Valencia, Los Angeles, Berkeley, Dartmouth, Buffalo, 1990–91. Published in <u>Places</u> 7, 3, 1991.

120

121

of much of Mies, but still through Mies, or so it seems to me, we get the 1949 house – something wholly original, wholly American. What is extraordinary is how, at a time when the American culture in its art-propaganda stance was very Europe-oriented, this house in Santa Monica seemed wholly free.

An Eames-defined territory, established by the pavilions set into it which reinforced the line of trees; with, on occupation, an Eames content. Seen from Europe it was something wonderful.

The framing, the skin, of the pavilions are a notation against which was played a content: both house and content perceived in graphic terms – an American phenomenon – to set in contrast with the very concrete, very European, Patio and Pavilion. The Eames' House and Patio and Pavilion° can be considered as phenomena in parallel.

In Patio and Pavilion, the vagueness of the images reflected back from the enclosing patio walls allowed a multitude of interpretations.°° The sense of completeness – territory, pavilion, objects of occupation[120, 121] – complete in the sense of walking into a house abandoned by the owners during the course of the evening meal, or into a ruined mine-working shut down by impending disaster and never re-opened. Patio and Pavilion is a picture of the art-processes of a period – thinking about it, the period of Becket/Dubuffet/Pollock/Brecht. The Eames House is a picture of the Eames.

° 'This is Tomorrow' exhibition, 1956, Whitechapel Art Galley, London.

°° The content – the objects of occupation – made or discovered by Nigel Henderson and Eduardo Paolozzi were of a richness and authenticity that no facsimile could catch.

December 1990, PS.

Formal influence on the Eames … the shapes used in the Eames-designed Arts and Architecture covers and for their chairs, plywood and moulded items, right up to the beginnings of the fifties were derived from those evolved by Hans Arp and Alexander Calder in the thirties. Circus is Calder/Leger in the US; Toys/Disneyland: the minusculisation, and the concentrated is a special quality.

Charles re-styled himself blue-collar. Ray never changed.

'Eames Dreams'.
Unpublished notes.

Winter 1990, PS.

In the <u>Black Book</u>° that catalogues all the Eames'
work there are two further houses … each seems
conventional to their period, each seems a product of drawing. The Santa Monica house is quite
other. Charles Eames was not a architect, he was
not a man of drawings.

In the Eames' House in Santa Monica, at the
point the decision was made to use the same steel
in a different way, that part of Eames' mind which
worked best, direct-working assembly, took-over. In
buildings it never happened again.

**On reading the
<u>Black Book</u>.
Unpublished.**

° John Neuhart,
Marilyn Neuhart,
Ray Eames, <u>Eames
Design</u>, Thames &
Hudson, London,
1989.

April 1991, PS.

All Eames' chair seats slope strongly upwards to   'Seat-Tilt'.
the front. It is this that gives them their sense of   Unpublished.
springiness, of bounce.

May 11 1991, PS.

On examination (in the Black Book°) the seat-tilt
insight proves to be largely true between 1945 and
1962. The seat-tilt, where measurable from flat-on
side photographs gives a 4-degree upward tilt for
plastic shells and 10 degrees for the wire shells.°°
This tilt certainly helps to give them their sense of
being new, being young, optimistic.

The Mies tubular, metal-framed chairs from
1926 had seats which were flat from front to back.

Bengt Akerblom, in his book Standing and Seat-
ing Posture,°°° gives a slope of seat 'if slippery' of
3–5 degrees.

Eames' chairs are also in dispute with Akerblom
about seat height. Akerblom gives 38–41 cm,
Eames 45 cm – the old before-the-war chair seat
height is maintained in Eames' chairs.

Eames' seat-tilt becomes gradually 'nor-
malised', that is, it varies from design to design.
After the sixties the chairs lose their absolute dis-
tinctiveness and bounce, lost perhaps to undue
pressure of the soft tissues of the posterior aspect
of the thigh?

'Seat-Tilt'.
Unpublished.

° Eames Design, op
cit, pages 52, 58,
97, 141, 153, 207,
227, 249, 275.

°° The lounge chair
has 15 degrees, but
this chair never had
any sense of
bounce, rather of
sag.

°°° Nordiska
Bokhandeln, 1948.

Appendix 1.
1959–60? PS.

'Eames Films',
possibly a lecture
for Architectural
Association
students since text
reproduced on
foolscap.
Unpublished.

Eames' films break into two groups: films in love with objects, the films themselves being as direct and self-contained as the object; and films out of love with objects, made as 'open sesames' to covetable ideas.

Of the films I have seen, the second group seems to start with the <u>Communications Primer</u>, 1953. This group all have sea-gulls in them.

It is easy to fall out of love with objects in a surfeit culture. Charles Eames himself tells of two hours spent in a new shopping place in Montreal – of the glut of toys, the hundreds of books, any one of which ten years ago would have seemed unbelievable. There was, he said, 'nothing to covet'. Now the essence of the covetable is that it is something out of reach and the world of mathematics and physics is out of reach for the Eames and therefore brings them to that special state of wonder necessary for their personal existence.

The format of these out-of-love-with-objects films is that of lessons, but they are palpably not real lessons, for if they were they would be much cooler and be part of a lesson sequence of a teaching programme. Whether they are effective 'open sesames' to the disciplines of the world of science is probably open to doubt. The Eames insist on the criteria that their films should not be embarrassing to the initiates in the disciplines they deal with. The film <u>Two Baroque Churches in Germany</u>, a 'lesson' film about Vierzenheilegen and Banz – where I can perhaps count myself as an initiate – seemed to me to be inadequate as to what these two churches are about. As a non-initiate the science films seem to teeter on a ridge between the banal and the whimsical. If it is a lesson one expects intellectual attack – the explanatory analogy to be as elegant as the idea being explained. If it is an 'object' film, it needs the uniqueness and consistency of the object explored.

My own explanation of the let-down of the later films and multi-projections is that the Eames themselves have not quite accepted (understood?) their relationship to the world of science – that of the

innocent eye – to permit their film to be as pure
statements of wonder about this world of ideas as
their earlier ones were of the world of the hand-
crafts of nineteenth-century America, of Japan,
Mexico, and India.

The Smithsons

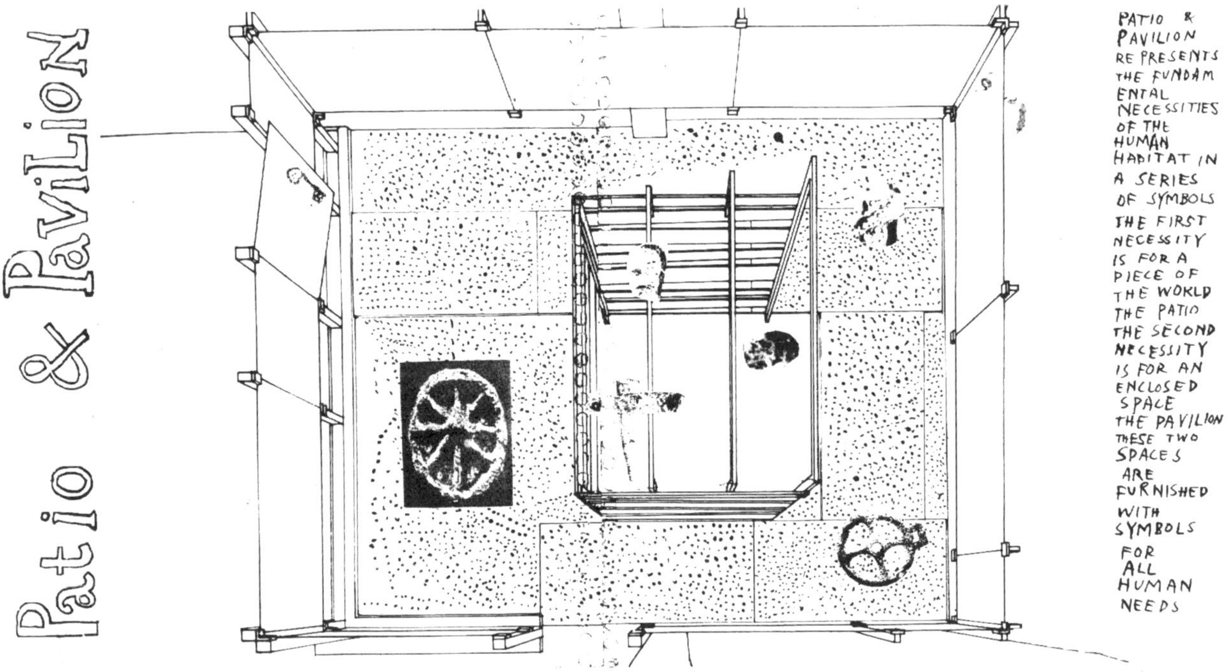

Patio & Pavilion

PATIO &
PAVILION
RE PRESENTS
THE FUNDAM
ENTAL
NECESSITIES
OF THE
HUMAN
HABITAT IN
A SERIES
OF SYMBOLS

THE FIRST
NECESSITY
IS FOR A
PIECE OF
THE WORLD
THE PATIO
THE SECOND
NECESITY
IS FOR AN
ENCLOSED
SPACE
THE PAVILION
THESE TWO
SPACES
ARE
FURNISHED
WITH
SYMBOLS
FOR
ALL
HUMAN
NEEDS

122

Summer 1956, PS.

123

124

In the group exhibit 'Patio and Pavilion' we worked on a kind of symbolic habitat in which are found responses, in some form or other, to the basic human needs – a view of the sky,[123, 124] a piece of ground, privacy, the presence of nature and of animals when we need them – to the basic human urges – to extend and control, to move. The actual form is very simple, a 'patio', or enclosed space, in which sits a 'pavilion'. The patio and pavilion[122] are furnished with objects which are symbols for the things we need: for example, a wheel image for movement and for machines.

The method of work has been for the group to agree on the general idea, for the architects to provide a framework and for the artists° to provide the objects. In this way the architects' work of providing a context for the individual to realise himself in, and the artists' work of giving signs and images to the stages of this realisation, meet in a single act, full of those inconsistencies and apparent irrelevances of every moment, but full of life.

'Patio and Pavilion' in the This is Tomorrow exhibition, Whitechapel Art Gallery, London, 1956, written for BBC Third Programme.

° Nigel Henderson, photograher; Eduardo Paolozzi, sculptor.

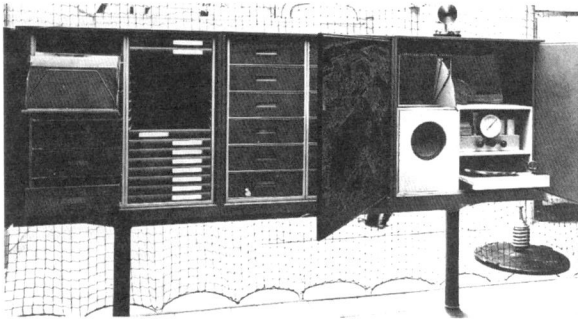

125

126

127

December 1957, AS.

'The Future of
Furniture',
Architectural
Design, April 1958,
Interior Design,
April 1958.

To both Purism and Bauhaus furniture was 'equipment', but for us, looking back over thirty years (from the end of the 1950s to the end of the 1920s), it is obvious that it was not really 'anonymous equipment' but furniture like in any other period. It was in the same aesthetic and carried the same idea as the architecture. Examples are the storage cabinets in the room for a young man in the Brussels Exhibition of 1935, which are specially designed to look like office equipment,[125] or the bank of storage in the Salon d'Automne Exhibition House of 1929, which look like fittings in an expensive lingerie shop.[126] For the architects of the twenties real 'anonymous equipment' hardly existed.[127] On the one hand things they selected –like the sink and white tiles – were craft objects retaining something from the unselfconscious phase of the industrial revolution. On the other hand, the appliances they chose – like cookers. with plain functional shapes° – were as much due to naiveté in the industry as to any desire for clean lines.

The kitchen of the Pioneer Modern Architect in Europe was very simple, with little equipment. But even in the twenties in the USA, appliances were posing an organisational problem. In 1930 the Brooklyn Gas Company got Lilian Galbraith to make a motion study in a ten-foot by twelve-foot kitchen. This study focused the attention of the public onto organisation, so both Europe and America were doing the same thing – the space between kitchen equipment was being reduced and the kitchen organisation made well-functioning.

In the 1950s stress was still laid on space and organisation, particularly by CIAM architects, yet the old forms for closed systems of organisation remained unchanged. Giedion typified the CIAM space man; in 1948 in his book Mechanisation Takes Command he was still writing of old rooms – kitchen, bathroom, dining room, and so on – whose organisation could always be improved by reviewing work processes.

Our generation were used to Le Corbusier being

° Bauhaus/Frankfort
designed gas
cookers an
exception.

128

able to give form to a changed situation. As one would expect, the 1946–52 Unité kitchen,[128] by Charlotte Perriand, was as much part of the architectural whole as were the pilotis and certainly had as great an impact on young architects as did the pilotis; but this was a re-styled kitchen which confused the issue for us in the fifties in Europe. In America the old European-type kitchen in the Farnsworth House, 1945–50, had the same effect.

In the twenties they had a mystique about the machine and consequently they played up their basic pieces of equipment; but in the late 1950s we tended to be crowded out by household appliances. Even within the concept of the mechanical core (within a Palladian organisation) the American kitchen and garage were likely to account for half the volume of the house. The architect had little control over these rooms whose walls are lined with appliances which would, over the years, so fundamentally change as to leave none of the original (architect-devised) space. The appliance industry fixed the dimensions and styling.°

Obviously it was necessary to find a method of dealing with the multitude of possibilities of combinations of appliances so that they could not obtrude their variously motivated aesthetics into the house space.

Twenty-five years after Lilian Galbraith's motion studies focused attention on well-functioning work spaces, appliances could do away altogether with the need of work space in this old sense. We could also assume that the large-sized appliance would soon become a thing of the past.

The change in concept was away from the adjusting pieces inside the room to a redistribution over the whole house, taking advantage of the flexibility or actual mobility the new appliances allowed.[129] Therefore we did not have more efficient rooms but a total shift out of the room fixation.

This was the basis of the Appliance House.

The Appliance House[130] gave the appliance def-

° Modular co-ordination of appliances would tend to narrow the field of choice and lessen still further the chance of control or approximation to what the architect wants.

SMALL PLEASURES OF LIFE

TO WORK OR WRITE AT A CREEPER BORDERED WINDOW

TO SEE THE SUNLIGHT SPREAD ACROSS THE FLOOR

TO STAND AND LOOK OUT WITHOUT GLARE

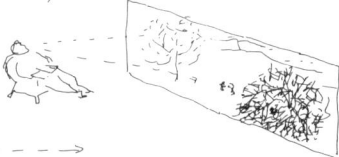

TO SEE THE VIEW / VEGETATION / TREES / THE GROUND WHILE SITTING

TO SEE OUT FROM THE BATHROOM OR PERHAPS BE LOVELY ENCLOSED

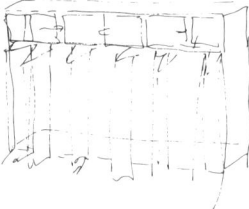

TO HAVE EASY ACCESS TO POSSESSIONS WITHOUT SENSING THEIR PRESENCE ALL THE TIME

TO READ IN BED

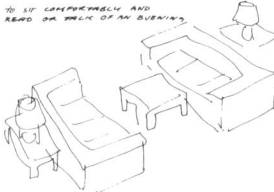

TO SIT COMFORTABLY AND READ OR TALK OF AN EVENING

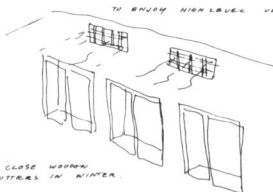

TO ENJOY HIGH LEVEL VENTILATION IN SUMMER

TO CLOSE WOODEN SHUTTERS IN WINTER.

129

130

inite areas in which to operate. The Appliance 'cubicles' contained all service connections, all storage, all equipment and appliances, and kept within the cubicle their noise, vibration and movement. The shell of the cubicle[131–133] formed the permanent structure defining the house space, while the inside could be stripped-out and re-equipped as owners/fashion/changing needs and methods demanded. Inside the cubicle, under control, the changing world of high-pressure advertising, styling and so on, plugged in, either in whole units, or built-up from assemblies of pre-fabricated parts, or whatever the market offered.

This changing part of houses, built facing in on itself, turned away from the house space proper which would be furnished very much as houses always have been, with a majority of moveable, placeable objects.

In the twenties, Purism, Bauhaus and de Stijl had their solid pieces of house equipment defining the spaces to which their light mobile furniture ('equipment') was related. But they were still furnishing the old rooms: bathroom and kitchen. From the 1950s there should be seen a change of orientation. To draw a parallel with the Japanese House: the storage unobvious to the spaces but defining them, contrary to the Western House which has tended towards displaying everything.[130]

The Appliance House was a move away from a furniture-appliance chaos towards a put-away house. The sort of furniture this house needed already existed, for the post-war period had produced its originals just as did the first period of Modern Architecture.* This post-war furniture had in fact pioneered the new mobility and the casual aesthetic.

* Constructivism is apparently without its chair, there being only the El Lizitsky Hygiene Exhibition (club reading room) chair of 1930, somehow under other — western? — influences.

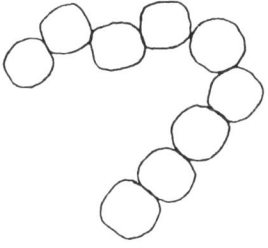

Entrance elevation

131

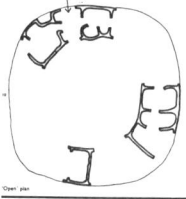

'Open' plan

'Closed' plan

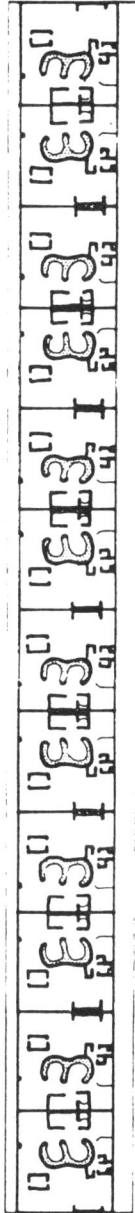

The Smithsons

113

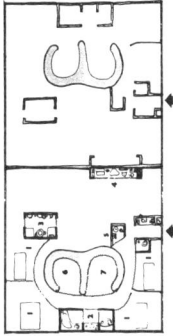

132

133

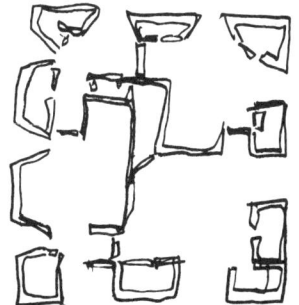

H.O.F.
PATIO HOUSE
'FOUGASSE LAYOUT'

134

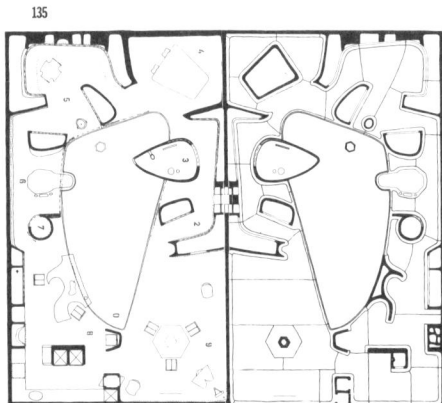

135

Spring 1958. PS.

"The Appliance House', Architectural Design, April 1958, Design 113, May 1958.

Generally people who buy appliances are just using them to prop up an existing way of life. The result is confusion. This postulates an alternative approach.

One of the fundamental tenets of the old Modern Architecture was the industrialisation of building, and in the absence of genuinely industrialised building techniques the architects of the twenties concerned themselves primarily with creating a formal language in the spirit of the machine. This language was no child of real technology.

However, what theoretical work was done on the problems of machine building has been the basis of much of the change that has subsequently taken place in the building industry, for example, in the fields of standard windows, precasting, and especially, in pre-fabrication.

Gropius' work at the Weissenhofseidlung in 1927 established the pattern of subsequent prefabrication – a panel system on a metre module. No fundamentally new thought entered the prefabrication field since that date. In general, prefabricators, following Gropius' lead, were always more interested in 'flexibility' than with the exact suitability to their functions of the internal spaces, or with the implications of the complete building in the community, or with the aesthetics of prefabrication. Their principal achievement continues to be producing building components under controlled conditions to reasonably high standards.

The flexibility offered by the stockyard – of standard-parts – has great intellectual appeal, but people handling these systems never seemed to have had the self-discipline or total idea to make out of the parts anything but the clumsiest sort of Meccano toy equivalent … and after our 1950s experience of the products of the systems, there was some doubt as to whether this sort of flexibility was worth having and that perhaps it would have been better to increase the size of units being standardised to at least the size of the whole house, or schools, or group, and to make such a unit available in several models. This would increase

136

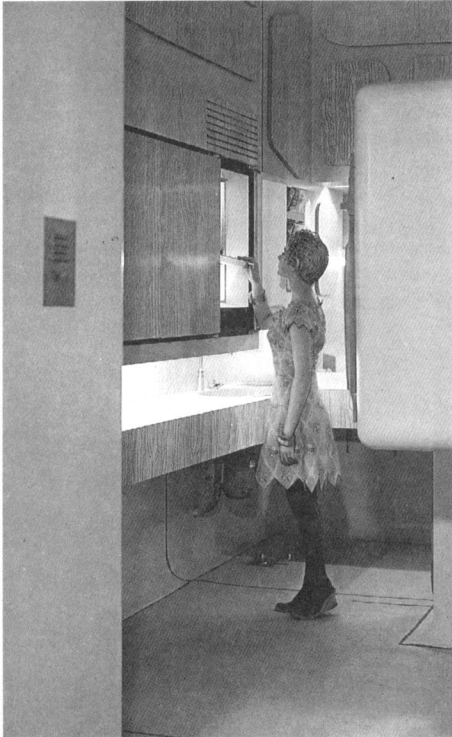

137

the range of choice and the chance of getting something which was really wanted from an industry sensitive to changes in social aspirations and style urges.°

Although the reasoning behind such an idea was to produce readily identifiable whole things, which in combination make the community easily comprehended, at the same time it went along with the technological desire for the elimination of random extras, uncontrolled variables and the simplification of maintenance.

There still seems no reason why such standard houses cannot have 'grouping characteristics' built into their design. For example the Ideal Home House of the Future,[134, 135] 1955–56, was designed to build up into a dense mass. And this point was overstated, so that the accepted idea – that a prefabricated house had to mean a detached house in a garden – was broken down.°°

The concept of the 'good-life' ever being sold by the symbol-manipulators is based on cars and domestic appliances, but this concept stops short of the house itself; appliance ads exist in a sort of never-never land, in a dustless, neigbourless, even childless, vacuum, where all that can be seen from the windows (if there are any) are spring trees and white clouds, not really declaring themselves as they really are, that is, as things that can revolutionise the life pattern: they are presented as convenient adjuncts to an old life pattern.

The approach by architects to the appliance-way-of-life is equally uncertain.°°° The House of the Future[136, 137] (for the working couple) tried to show the architectural consequences of – among other things – the disintegration of the kitchen by prepackaging, food treatment, mobile appliances and so on. The house was designed – like a car – as one thing, for a limited role. But in a family house the problems are different from a car, where only a few things can be eliminated without destroying the performance. In a house there are many variables, the removal of some or the changing of many of them would not fundamentally alter

° Rather like the American car industry in its affluent years.

°° This is not to say that the isolated house in a garden is an invalid concept, only that it can be invalidated by certain circumstances – for example, when the spaces between are so small as to be useless, or ideologically, should a counter-concept of the good-life be presented.

°°° For example, the Monsanto plastic house, which in spite of its advanced technology, is old style in ts plan concept, in its use of equipment and shape of things.

the performance. Therefore a house designed like a car is at some disadvantage, for the fittings would be so closely integrated into the space-structure concept that to change the refrigerator would be like getting a bigger glove compartment in a Volkswagen dashboard – it is easier to get a new car.°

It would seem that there are two possibilities for a technological building industry. The first, to produce limited-role whole-units, preferably throwaway – which implies maximum number production without variation. The second, mass production of components (bricks, sheet materials, hinges, baths, service assemblies, and so on) combined with the use of multiple-function automation machines to produce specials in small runs. These things would be assembled in a unique way like old craft buildings.

Whichever technique the architect chooses, his function is to propose a way of life and the appliance-way-of-life suggests an entirely new sort of house.°°

° And of course, in the situation of a city, where a choice of dwellings is available, a change of house would also be normal.

°° Housing Committees would not accept any sort of industrialised or prefabricated dwelling as these were felt to be simply fobbing-off the workers with something that the middle classes would not have. To be acceptable a council house had to represent in minature the craft-built suburban villa.

138

139

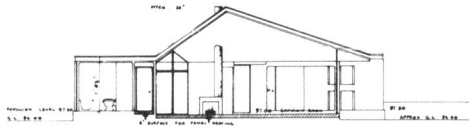

1958, PS.

'Techniques and Technology', given as the last of a series of talks to students at the Architectural Association School, London, published in The Architects' Journal, 21 May 1959.

More and more, mass-production techniques change our ways of living and of thinking without the consent of the traditional avant-garde – the artists and intellectuals and their patrons. Innovation – or change of style – now enters society horizontally from mass-production industry and its ad-men, with feedback into the old fine arts.

In this situation it is necessary to change the whole focus of fine-art architectural activities; to produce powerfully distinct alternatives. For example, a desirable alternative must be offered to the private estate developers' house, a new popular image with all the kick that the Tudorbethan semi-detached had in the thirties. We have to invent a house capable of mass production, or using mass production components and having built into its organisation a method of grouping house with house, to give a new urban pattern: one which accepts the car with the same grace as the houses in Bath accepted the carriage.[138, 139]

The relationship between the means and the architecture is the same as that of words of common speech with poetry. In the same way, once these means have been used distinctly, the 'anonymous' becomes specific, has been given special meaning.

It is possible that a future architecture will be expendable and that an urban discipline of a few fixed points and a scatter of change will develop. In such an architecture the shortness of life can allow of solutions in which the first process is the last process. There would be no problem of maintenance. At present most buildings are assumed to be permanent and consequently, as their materials require maintenance if they are to survive, the problems of maintenance must be a factor in their evolution.

Many buildings adopting industrial or pseudo-industrial techniques (such as curtain walling) produce surfaces so complex and in so many materials that their fabric was almost impossible to maintain. The painting of some small surfaces, the oiling of others, and the wire-wool cleaning of others, if difficult, is bound to be neglected, and ultimately, the building's aesthetic of complication invalidated. Probably this is a penalty paid for transferring techniques from, say, the motor industry, which is concerned with a two- to ten-year unmaintenanced body-work life, to buildings which are usually conceived as having a life of many human generations.

Summer 1959, AS.

'Caravan: Embryo Appliance House?', Architectural Design, September 1959.

Caravans are the nearest to an expendable architecture that the market has to offer and it would appear by their popularity that people are prepared to put up with some conditions more primitive than those their grandmothers knew – mud outside the door, children in a field which is at the mercy of the English climate – to achieve greater gains; that of the caravan providing a home of one's own at the right time, at the right price, with little or no outlay on furnishings, and a home which is technological, twentieth-century, new. Caravans obviously provide a solution for a lot of people who – perhaps only temporarily – do not want bye-law streets or a garden city set-up. For against the standard solution of the permanent dwelling, the caravan is neat, like a big piece of equipment; has a place for everything, like a well-run office; has miniature appliances in scale with the space, like a toy home; is as comfortable as this year's space-heated car, and like the car, the caravan presents a new freedom.

Partly because of its styling, the caravan has become a sort of symbol as well as a sign of a population in flux. It no doubt has something of the cheerful, safely transient feeling one gets driving along in a car, remote from the craftsman class of 1917 the Garden City idea was meant for.

Not so easy to separate from mere acceptance of what the market offers, but supported by what appears desirable as acquisitions, it would also seem that certain miniaturising trends in equipment are very acceptable to a new class of couples, childless couples, or young-in-spirit-elderly whose children have left home.

In this, as a form of dwelling almost as much as in its appliance-conscious bias, the caravan contains a much greater potential as a possible pointer to a new basic 'parent's cell' embodying and implying a new way of life, than anything else. However the caravan site offers no pointer to the look of the new environment any more than the outside of the caravan or the interior styling does the new architectural form of the cell. But it is at this

level that ordinary permanent housing most significantly fails. Yet the caravan in its very primitiveness can make us re-examine the premises for all the expensive miles of estate roads, the street lighting along these miles, acres of tiny gardens all requiring fencing of some sort, the endless repetition of daily household tasks, medieval in their waste of each individual's time and energy, not to mention the waste of natural resources. We must question whether the brick permanent house, which we are perpetuating at great expense in initial cost plus subsidies, is what the new class of technicians (to take only one section of the community) really wants.[140]

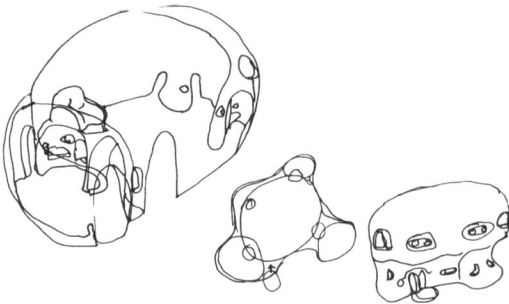

140

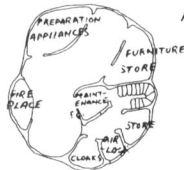

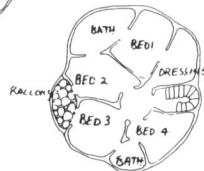

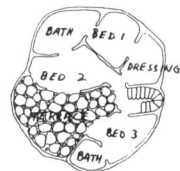

APPLIANCE HOUSE 1 — 'BREAT HOUSE
NOV 57

UPPER FLOOR

4 BED

3 BED + TERRACE

May 1964, PS.

From this week° it is possible for the first time to walk into a shop°° and buy a Breuer chair. This is very nice – even Breuer himself claimed in 1962 that he had managed to get one made exactly as the original design in San Francisco only the previous year. It is forty years too late and that lateness presents us with a problem.

Is a reproduction Breuer, or a Le Corbusier (available in Switzerland) or a reproduction Barcelona (long available in the USA) any less false than a reproduction Chippendale or Louis Quinze? They suffer the same 'errors' – they have been modified to suit later tastes and different technologies. The base of the Corb chaise longue is not the original; the Breuer chair has leather strap-work; there is even talk in the Mies office of Tughendat chairs in stainless-steel tube (not nickel-plated steel).

All very practical changes, but no different from the change of wood, the use of machine tools, which it was held made reproductions of seventeenth- and eighteenth-century chairs unacceptable to the apologists of modern design in the thirties. Furthermore, they are reproduced for exactly the same reasons, they were the 'master pieces' of an epoch – in reproduction beautiful objects in themselves and capable of evoking the Golden Age which produced them.

Le Corbusier of course used 'antique' furniture in his 1920s projects – Thonet chairs designed in the 1880s or 1890s and square English leather club chairs of unknown antiquity – but they were machine pop objects in current production and rationalised as such. No such programmatic prop is available to ease our conscience – all the chairs we are talking about are deliberate revivals of old designs, reproductions in the traditional sense.

I myself feel no special revulsion. The problem is intellectual. Indeed I experience no distaste for any reproduction furniture or for old Williamsburg architecture. It is even vaguely enjoyable – like the fact that Downing Street has gone and Old Williamsburg has appeared, modified to suit contemporary taste, so it is not really anywhere – but

'Reproduction Furniture', written as by Waldo Camini as a 'Not Quite Architecture' for The Architects' Journal, but published in Architectural Review, August 1964.

° Article in The Sunday Times, 3 May 1964.

°° Aram Designs, Kings Road, London.

I am still not revolted, only sad and reflective.

Nevertheless, in my dining room I'll stick with Eames, for in my heart of hearts I still think to choose otherwise is cultural cowardice in the face of the enemy.

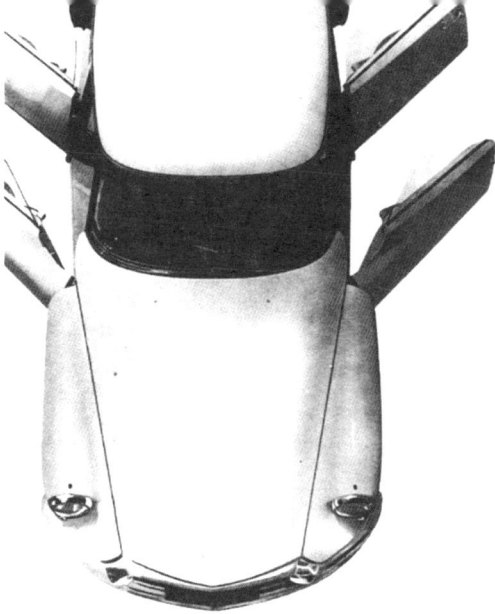

141

142

143

10 December 1963,
tailpiece 15 January
1964, revised 14
June 1966, PS.

Thinking about the Economist Building, we have become aware that a logical shift has taken place in our attitude towards mechanicals and services. We have at the same time begun to understand the reasons for our enjoyment of Citröen/Braun design mode.[141–143]

'Concealment and Display: Meditations on Braun', published in <u>Architectural Design</u>, July 1966.

The services and mechanicals in a large building, the range of needs to be served, the unpredictability of the styling of the casings of quite simple things like switch gear, thermostats, and so on, all tend to produce a confused jumble which speaks not at all about what they are doing. And what are they doing? Only producing light and air and disposing of waste products.

Lighting as a fitting is an acceptable idea in the farmhouse kitchen, the bulb and shade are symbols of the bright lights and the pavements of the city – but five hundred of them in an office building is ridiculous.

So it is with the radiator; one in a room is a substitute for a fire, something to stand by – but five thousand in a hospital is coelacanthic – like being a prisoner in the nineteenth century.

Ambient light, ambient air, no fuss about detail, awareness in a quiet way that the sweetness of functioning is architecture. In a large building it involves us with the organising of mechanicals and services with a clear formal objective in mind, for, as Louis Kahn said, the suspended ceiling speaks about nothing; not of the services it hides, not of the structure which is above it, not of what it is made, not of the space below. It speaks about nothing.

In a real building, the light and the space and the air are one. Sniff the air, sense the space, know how to act. How to keep this sense of what is going on – where the light and air are coming from, how to get in and out, where the pipes run and where the lifts travel – that is the question.

In the Economist Building the answer seems to be: a simple plan with an obvious services core, a suppression of the pipe-work with an easily-read hierarchy of access panels from the sealed tight to the readily accessible; doors to walk through that cannot be confused with cupboards; light, on the whole, being made just to seem to be around; air arriving and departing obviously but unobtrusively; and the arrangement of the storage and work areas so that they indicate their intended use. In a roundabout way one has arrived at a certain conclusion concerning repetition and number – what we were all worrying about at CIAM 9 at Aix-en-Provence in 1953. At the time it seemed to be one of the most important things discussed there, but all subsequent exploration of number patterns and size of social groupings seemed to get nowhere.

Suddenly it would seem that one of the things that is crucial to large numbers and to repetition is a special sort of anonymity of styling – a conclusion no-one would have dared even think about in 1953 – and this is an important and civilising realisation.

17 July 1970, PS

Review of
'Exhibition of
Modern Chairs,
1918–70', at the
Whitechapel Art
Gallery, London.
Published in
Architectural
Design, September
1970.

The only thing now available to designers which was not there in the Heroic Period is moulded plastic.

By the modern tradition one would expect the language appropriate to a new mood and a new material to be definitively established in a chair. It would seem that Jo Columbo's chair 64860 might be it.[144]

145

146

Winter 1970, PS.

'Signs of Occupancy', lecture written for seminar Wittwatersrand, Easter 1970, published Plan, Vol. 56 No. 8, August 1971; Architectural Design, February 1972.

The ideal house is that which one can make one's own without altering anything. Make one's own in the usual way, that is, within the limits of the fashion of the time and without feeling any pressure either to communicate one's trivial uniqueness or to conform absurdly.

That this is possible scarcely needs demonstrating in England. The most casual walk in Kensington or Bath[144, 145] offers a look through open doors into an elegant hall or a lacoaon of rusting prams; the sounds floating out of upper windows; lights on to lined curtains or the old 40-watt bulb over a pensioner's tea; the smell of flowers, or old fat, or cats. The richness of the mix within an apparently static format is incredible.

The search for a style which can match this ideal has been the floating centre of our effort – certainly since the mid-Economist years – and explains the mulling-over of the Eames House and our close watching of the gradually evolving subtly modulated façades of late Mies.

What we would seem to be looking for is the gentlest of styles, which whilst still giving an adumbration of the measures of internal events and structures – rooms, activities, servicing arrangements, supports – leaves itself open to – even suggests – interpolation, without itself being changed.

In the old farms around Florence or Parma, one can see from what base the architecture of the Renaissance sprang. It came from well thought-out, solidly-built farms. Their organisation was such that rural occupations could be separated from brute labour and be seen as capable of perfection – of becoming pleasures and ideas. Out of these farms the country villa became a fundamental word in the form-language of three centuries, around which successive styles gathered their meanings.

One of the few to talk in terms of the form-language of the Heroic Period of modern architecture, both as indicator and as enhancement of everyday use, was Rex Martienssen.

A visual description, such as that made by Mar-

147

148

tienssen for the Cité de Refuge, 1929–33 by Le Corbusier, of a sequence of 'preparations for entry',[147, 148] could be matched by a description of the same sequence by the guided hand, or by a description of the experience of the way trodden by the foot; for the whole body is involved.

That we should accept that the things we are likely to touch should be as if pre-smoothed by the human hand, that things near to us should be flawless and undisturbing, even pretty, that all materials and their handing should indicate and enhance use, seems reasonable.

But it is difficult for us to allow ourselves to think like this, for the Modern Movement as a movement was puritanical – equating the hard with the good – and it was committed to attitudes which because of the force of the founders we find difficult and unnatural to shake off. For example, the Modern Movement was committed to solving the problems of the many, it accepted the idea of standardisation to produce the numbers that mass-production demanded; for the Modern Movement at that time only mass-production – then also in its heroic phase – could solve the problems of the many.

That with standardisation a certain inarticulateness, imprecision and even inconvenience, could be involved it accepted for the greater good and because, more importantly to it then, standardisation really spoke of l'esprit nouveau.

In the 1990s machine processes can achieve the profiles and the degree of smoothness or hardness which use requires, rather than imposing limitations.

That the degree of finish could tell us things was already spelled out in the early fifties by Le Corbusier's Unité at Marseilles with its 'container' rough (the urban framework) and the 'contained' well-finished (the house-cell); and in Chicago by Mies van der Rohe's 860 Lake Shore Drive with its understated public face and with places one can make one's own inside. Not that we thought about those buildings in this way when they were new – it is through the old Disneyland in Los Angeles and,

149

more recently, Port Grimaud, which are so unashamedly pleasure-indicating places that one suddenly begins to think differently.

Much of the form-language used at Port Grimaud is not available to us because the underlying uses cannot survive outside the very artificial circumstances of a rich-man's play town. For example, the articulation of the street pattern, its shaping and enlivening with small shops and cafés with appropriate widenings of the largely vehicleless wall-to-wall streets cannot be transposed. Those shops and cafés serve tourists and residents there to enjoy themselves – to buy at smart shops and eat in expensive cafés is part of the summer enjoyment. These things are special to the situation. These shops flourish.

But in the circumstances of ordinary urban housing the number of small shops is few, cafés fewer. In fact the whole marketing trend of the industrialised countries is towards larger and fewer shops.

Larger and fewer means big-vehicle served and acres of customer car-parking. The average supermart is a lot less enjoyable than the average tractor-parts factory, therefore where there is real affluence the small shop re-invents itself as a delicatessen or speciality shop. But for the less affluent there are inevitably yards and yards of just houses with no ready-made easy means with which to articulate, to enliven.

But this should not frighten us. There are few corner-shops in Bath, but many hundreds of yards of just houses as liveable and relaxed as any anywhere and this is achieved through a rich and flexible form-language entirely based on the use house – houses/street/service street/service yards/service buildings/gardens/houses' ground.[149]

As the builders of Bath decided that the terrace-house form would work for them, we think that for city housing the street-deck form will serve. It is, we feel, a solidly established form capable of being articulated through its sub-forms towards a liveable and relaxed 'ideal-house'.

What we have tried to do in the development of

150

151

152

153

154

the basic idea (connected street-decks giving choice of approach, choice of companions; clearly stated groups of dwellings for mutual social support; adequate 'door-steps' to protect and identify dwellings within the group)[150–154] is to evolve the form and sub-forms so as to indicate clearly how the place is to be used. So that its occupiers are left in no doubt, yet be unaware of having been told, which is intended to be the quiet part and which is noisy, where one is expected to walk and where to drive, where to play, where to deliver or bring the ambulance. The form-language of the building to indicate and enhance use.

At Robin Hood Gardens the street-deck is clearly for horizontal movement; lifts are shafts of vertical movement; where deck and shaft meet is a definite place. The street-deck itself is articulated so that the part by the individual front doors offers itself for being taken possession of by the householder.

The dwellings are stated as enclosures but the exact internal use left open to interpretation to reflect the interchangeable use of rooms that ordinary dwellings require.

Vehicle movement is kept in a moat, visibly and obviously below ground level. A moat which contains the noise and holds the heavier-than-air vehicle fumes below the level of the dwellings and the people-occupied open spaces. And so on.

We have tried to evolve the form-language to indicate and enhance use.

Concrete near the eye is smooth and moulded to be self-cleaning and neat – able to be touched.

Concrete far from the eye is coarser – it is concrete to be passed-by not lived with.

Joinery to be touched has smoothly rounded edges and is made of excellent timber of straight knot-free grain – inviting further waxing and polishing.

Where much wear or weather is expected timber is protected by paint, glossy – suggesting wiping down, re-painting. And so on.

Written down all this seems so banal that one

155

156

157

158

wonders quite why it is worth saying; but in spite of it having been normal to all Europe since the rise of the Burgher cultures in the 1400s, it is not common today for a form-language to be based on common use and the pleasures of common use.

In the Heroic Period J J P Oud's De Kiefhoek in Rotterdam,[155–158] an ordinary municipal housing estate, was built from the bottom up with a love that is still shiningly obvious. Every bit of wood and length of tube is as deliberately shaped and placed as any in the old houses of Delft or Gouda. Each change of road width, every set-back is made to speak of use. Yet in our terms, De Keifhoek is mass-housing on the smallest budget. Oud built within the common technology of his time, for the social ethos of his time – surely the facing up to the invention of a form-language of common use for our period cannot be any more difficult than it was for Oud.

Charles Eames said that design could only touch India if it was carried into every village through something universally used. To evolve a form-language for the architecture of an industrialised society on the basis of the pleasures of use is perfectly possible.

Verbal illustration 1
to 'Singns of
Occupancy'.

159

Of Le Corbusier's Salvation Army (La Cité de Refuge) in Paris[159] Martienssen said:° 'The purpose of a Refuge involves a continuously changing population; it is at one and the same time a monument, a focal point and a hotel. We are not concerned at present with the general working arrangement (gateway, porch, bridge, vestibule), there is a graded succession of enclosing or limiting stages that may be categorised as Constructivist. The whole scheme, entrance, distribution, dormitories, dining rooms, workshops, stands out from its drab surroundings with the crystalline purity and the monumental attribute is established in a powerful yet elementary geometry. By the very nature of its treatment, with the broad south-facing façade of light and the vigorous polychromy of the tall entrance porch, the Cité de Refuge becomes a focal point for those whom it welcomes. The multiple requirements are exactly adjusted to an extremely unpromising site. The bulk accommodation stands out boldly and clearly in simple forms, but the approach – the adequate liaison between the inhospitable street and ultimate protection – is achieved with greater complexity, with judgement and sensibility finding a free satisfaction on the hyper-practical plane. This graded approach is visually penetrated from the street and provides a transition whose change of direction and elasticity of volume are capable of introducing a high degree of sensible experience. The gateway of wire mesh encloses but does not obscure a small forecourt from which a short flight of steps carries one to a lofty, partially open porch of strictly cubic intention, whence a change of direction brings one, at a higher level, across a bridgeway to the circular vestibule.

'A description is necessarily inadequate to convey what are essentially experiences of movement and perception, but it is suggestive to compare such a modulated penetration with the more common blunt entry into an isolated volume without transition in our own time. The Egyptians, Greeks and Romans were meticulous in providing for small

° 'Constructivism and Architecture', South African Architectural Record, July 1941.

works an ample zone of adjustment.'

To talk of wire mesh in this way as one would of a seventeenth-century bronze screen in a Cairo mosque might seem ludicrous, but in fact what is described is what it really did. Le Corbusier's sensibility raised it from a necessity into one of the pleasures of use.

Verbal illustration 2
to 'Signs of
Occupancy'.

'What to do about
design in India, The
Eames' Ford
Foundation report
to the Government
of India, 1958'; part
of an extract
published in
Architectural
Design, September
19??

'Of all the objects we have seen and admired during our visit to India, the lota, that simple vessel of everyday use, stands out as perhaps the greatest, the most beautiful – the village women have a process which, with the use of tamarind and ash,each day turns this brass into gold.

'But how would one go about designing a lota?

'First one would have to shut out all preconceived ideas on the subject and then begin to consider factor after factor: the optimum amount of liquid to be fetched, carried, poured, and stored in a prescribed set of circumstances.

'The size and strength and gender of the hands (if hands) that would manipulate it.

The way it is to be transported: head, hip, hand, basket, or cart.

'The balance, the centre of gravity, when empty, when full, its balance when rotated for pouring. The fluid dynamics of the problem not only when pouring, but when filling and cleaning, and under the complicated motions of head carrying – slow and fast.

'Its sculpture as it fits the palm of the hand, the curve of the hip.

'Its sculpture as complement to the rhythmic motion of walking or a static pose at the well.

'The relation of opening to volume in terms of storage uses – and objects other than liquid.

'The size of the opening and inner contour in terms of cleaning.

'The texture inside and out in terms of cleaning and feeling.

'Heat transfer: can it be grasped if the liquid is hot?

'How pleasant does it feel, eyes closed, eyes open?

'How pleasant does it sound when it strikes another vessel, is set down on ground or stone, empty or full – or being poured into?

'What is the possible material?

'What is its cost in terms of working?

'What is its cost in terms of ultimate service?

'What kind of an investment does the material

provide, as product, as salvage?

'How will the material affect the contents, etc. etc.?

'How will it look as the sun reflects off its surface?

'How does it feel to possess it, to sell it, to give it?

'No one man designed the lota, but many men over many generations. Many individuals represented in their own way through something they may have added or may have removed, or through some quality of which they are particularly aware.'

Interpreting Eames: form-language sets up a dialogue between object and user. The object suggests how it can be used, the user responds by using it well – the object improves; or it is used badly – the object is degraded, the dialogue ceases.

It can of course revive for there is a secret and permanent life in things intensely made that can come alive for other uses, other generations – even when the damage is extremely severe, even when only a ruin or a fragment is left. But in its first period of life the object must have love, or at least regard.

160

161

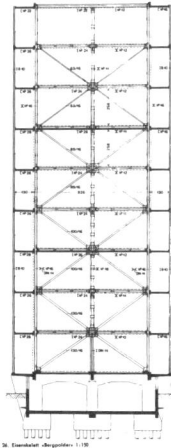

162

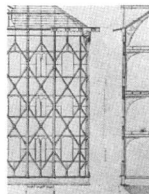

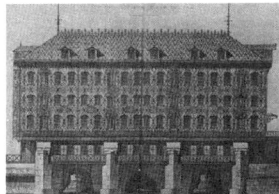
163

18 January 1974, PS.

'To Embrace the Machine', published in Architectural Design, April 1974.

In the years around 1932 a change took place in Modern Architecture; the Heroic Period ended, something new began.

Perhaps to say something new began is wrong, for the impulse to embrace the machine has never gone away. The Romans discovered that logical organisation and clear repetitive construction produced a beauty and a satisfaction all its own. The pleasures of the Rue de Rivoli are Roman pleasures; as are those of the Demoiselle,[160] the Crystal Palace, and the Boots Factory. Owen Williams' Boots Factory at Beeston is from 1930–32; 1932 is the date of construction of Le Corbusier's Immeuble Clarté[161] in Geneva. Van Tijen, Brinkmann and Van der Vlugt built the Bergpolder flats[162] in 1933–34; Beaudoin and Lods their Ecole en Plein Air in 1935–36.

There were of course marvellous works of that time which still spoke, but with a changed accent, the language of the twenties. But underlying one of these – Le Corbusier's Pavilion Suisse in Paris, also from 1930–32 – was the wildly extravagant and dotty Menier Chocolate Factory[163] over the Marne, the consequence of what can be called the 'engineer's impulse'.

This engineer's impulse is not a question of functionalism, but of another obsession, an obsession with making the idea of the structure speak clearly in accordance with its engineer's inner picture, no matter what difficulties have to be overcome to bring this about, which accounts for the quirkiness, the intensity.°

The examples from the 1930s of buildings which had embraced the machine – the Boots Factory, Immeuble Clarté, Bergpolder, Ecole en Plein Air – are all taken from Alfred Roth's immediately postwar book The New Architecture of 1946. To me then, all the buildings in that book were modern; I could not distinguish between those that inherited their formats and style from the Heroic Period and those which had truly embraced the machine.

This new period was consequent on the extent of the need for housing and 'social equipment'

° Which attracts us to the work of Eiffel. Something of this spirit was at work in the 1970s, for example in Candillis, Josic, Woods, Schiedhelm's Free University in Berlin, 1973, and SOM's Handcock Tower in Chicage, 1970. In both of those works one is at once aware of a quality we cannot easily interpret.

164

165

which stared serious architects in the face and a growing mastery of technique, but was most of all the consequence of a resurgence of the feeling that problems were solvable.°

Jean Prouvé, a survivor from the thirties, when this feeling was most intense, took up again the theme he laid aside in 1939 in the development studies for the Free University in Berlin. Sheet-steel flat-looking double-sided skin panels to be hung on to the explicitly separate steel frame (with similar-looking moveable partitions inside). This had been the theme of his Maison du Peuple at Clichy,[164, 165] built in 1938/39 with architects E Beaudoin and M Lods with V Bodiansky – a building so radical it is amazing it ever got built. But there it is, secure, reticent, eloquent, and detailed with an assurance and a bravado that Eiffel himself would have found hard to match.[167]

166

° It was with this energy and optimism that the nineteenth century also had embraced the machine.

25 January 1974.
Verbal illustration to
'To Embrace the
Machine'.

At first sight, Roth's book The New Architecture amounted to a puzzle as to the nature of the commonality of the selected buildings ... all clean, white, pure in their ways, mostly by architects who looked like well-shaven Latin American bankers. The reason for the choice seemed then, the late forties, that each building was well-intentioned; that here were works by committed architects (almost like priests); and here was the standard of decency that should be achieved by reasonable men. Looking again at the book, the work still speaks of this, and so doing must still encourage those who do the work they put their name to.

But at the start of the fifties, the Britain Can Take [Fake] It exhibition demonstrated all too clearly to those young then that good intentions were not enough; there had again to be style, and a concomitant commitment to what style stood for; this was what basically separated most of Team 10 from most of CIAM – for many members of CIAM attended both it and the IUA for seemingly no better reasons than both were international (and reform is always the spear – and shield – of middle-men).

It is again possible to see thirties styling in quantity in the shops; I still know it is not what we are after. Yet I like the buildings in Roth's book. Roth's thirties had their own kind of calm, cool, neutral, stood-off stance; elsewhere there may have been stainless steel; all shades of North African colouring – beige through chocolate – and many, many, other still very attractive aspects: but BIBA's thirties (and forties) brings it all back;° the confrontation. Not what we were after, not what we are now after. What revolted then, what we pitied – yes, pitied – the middle generation for was their vacuousness, their Waugh/Maugham/Green/Duff-Cooper stigmata of uselessness, their idolising of parasitism, their not-worth-holding attitudes to life. These strangely arid qualities – one imagines like the glass of champagne drunk in the cigarette staleness after last night's party – are still in the resurrected objects and newly prized buildings: for

° BIBA was a shop that grew in London in the sixties: the period of swinging London (the Beatles, Twiggy, and so on).

those on reconnaissance for what might be, such an atmosphere is still the malady of culture; the slithery enemy of true change; the befuddlement of purpose.

The cool of the seventies is more stood-off, with reason replacing snobbery; at best, a wary nostalgia after seeming innumerable wars; a self-sufficient light-heartedness in the sense of sheer survival (this of course forties CIAM had; except they had all survived more, Nazi Europe in many cases). If one is an objective observer of the pool of ideas to be dipped into, both the conceit of snobbishness and free-wheeling of historic revival are disallowed.

Spring 1975, PS.

'Making the
Connection',
Architectural
Design, May 1975.

We have previously argued that an architecture that can awaken a sun, nature, climate, aspect-prospect consciousness in its inhabitants, makes the necessary base-connection on which the collective design impulse depends for its start. What is being said here is that, by tradition, the architect's other work is with the generalised theoretical base and the language. And for the machine-supported, present-day cities, only a live, cool, highly controlled, rather impersonal architectural language can deepen that base connection, make it resonate with the culture as a whole ... give it meaning within meaning, give it a history and a continuity within modern architecture, for modern architecture was intended both as an affirmation of an older dream of a machine-civilisation and a cry of joy at an actual arrival.

There are two buildings from the Heroic Period of modern architecture which demonstrably make a connection at both the real and the ideal levels – Le Corbusier's Villa à Garches and Mies van der Rohe's Tugendhat House. At the Garches Villa it is quite clear which is the sun side and which is the shadow, where one should drive and where one should walk-in, where one should look out and where the garden is. It makes these real connections through an ideal architectural language, a language which in fact it was there and then establishing. Yet seen at this distance, it seems already miraculously generalised and available in exactly the same sense as the classical language of architecture. Some of these things, some similar things, can be said about the Tugendhat House.

Yet modern architecture as it spread in the thirties, except in a handful of buildings, registered only the excitement of the signalling of the arrival of the machine-civilisation. Architects, long-bred out of an intellectual tradition, did not recognise that the machine-aesthetic has a base in a developing doctrine. It was not until the late forties and fifties, when Mies van der Rohe himself began to underscore the generalised theoretical base on which his work was established and growing and

his work itself simplified to a point where at least its underlying organisational principles were easily available, that modern architecture as the beginning of an architecture became recognised.

Our generation inherited the Heroic Period and the To Embrace the Machine Period of the Modern Movement, and had to extend it to new moods. It had to inspect the real face of the machine-culture, which is not that which the originating generation saw as an act of imagination and invention. That machine-culture seems now to call for an effort of connection to extend at both the real and the ideal levels.

To trigger the impulse to collective design, it is connection at the real level that seems critical: for the inhabitants to know without conscious thought where to offer their abilities ... to dress, to plant, to play, to drive, to clean, to innovate, to manage for themselves and their group. The possibilities for all these direct, real connections seem to have been neglected in all but the rarest places and for that real connection to be deepened through the resonance of an architecture with its base in machine-culture is rarer still.[167]

168

169

170

Autumn 1985, AS.

The dictionary definition of 'idyll' is as follows: a description of a picturesque scene or incident, especially in rustic life; an episode suitable for such treatment.

These three pavilions[168–170] embody the idyll as a place wherein to be restored to oneself; as a source of one's energies. The pavilion is thus seen as a place made idyll; a dream of a stress-free way of life, a domain – often a greater garden – often in the pretend wild; that is, in nature.

All three pavilions are effective form-inventions for the place in nature: the fragment of a would-be enclave, whose integrity relies on the decent behaviour of others. In the St Jerome sense,[*] a study from which to appraise, contemplate, consider, re-assess, the city.

Of the three pavilions, two have been made uninhabitable as idyll, by noise. The first, because of a State highway's new bridge, virtually directed at the site, with a significant increase in traffic during the 1950s and 1960s, together with a camping site on the opposite bank of the river. It therefore has its second owner.

The second pavilion is lived in by its original inhabitant. It is in a backland, on a ledge at the end of the Hollywood Hills, above the Pacific. The drop to the beach road allows the house to be in an acoustic shadow (it is backed against the hill; being pulled back from the brink of the ledge's drop at the last moment, when the steel was already on site). The traffic and beach-use noise has increased dramatically since the late 1940s but on the ledge it is heard as a sort of oceanic roar that the expansive view of the ocean excuses.

The third also has its second owner, because the conjoined territory of the minuscule cluster of the enclave within farm land, turned user-unfriendly; that is, it became occupied by mechanical cowboys.

The pavilion called the Farnsworth House was built for Dr Edith Farnsworth by Mies van der Rohe, 1945–50. A clandestine visit was made by PS in 1958. Twenty-six years later, in 1984, a second

'Three Pavilions of the Twentieth Century: the Farnsworth, the Eames, Upper Lawn', a lecture given in connection with the seminar 'A Fragment of an Enclave', held in Barcelona, November, 1985.

[*] Hironymous/Saint Jerome: The Desert, The Study, Tecta, Lauenförde, 1991.

171

173

owner, and, in late autumn, a short stay by A and PS

The second pavilion was made by Charles and Ray Eames for their home and studio in 1949. In the early 1950s, a long strip poster, black line on chalk white, announced the Eames' Wire Chair series and amid illustration of the mesh of the legs was poised a knowing blackbird.[172] The bird still lives in his pavilion with his prototype wire chairs, of which he is justly proud.

The territory of the bird is the plateau.

Quite a friendly bird.

Custodian bird: the bird's beady eye sees us off his territory.

We leave the bird to his Idyll.

The Folly/Solar Pavilion at Upper Lawn, Wiltshire, is the third. We photographed at first rarely, then, gradually, the cameras were taken down more often; at first related to season, or expected outing; latterly because we saw in it different aspects of our life.[171, 173–177]

With the doors open the yard flowed through the pavilion. The pavilion sat in the walled yard and garden as in an enclave, the view was its domain.

The pavilion had no rights of protection beyond its wall.

It was lived in at first camp-style, its decoration the as-found.

On wet days we read. Gradually the standard of comfort was increased and the amount of light for evenings.

The view was about 300 degrees around.

The yard and garden, because of the wall, was an enfolding outdoor room.

The weather of the penultimate February weekend was moist, quiet, enclosing.

Territory is necessary to support the pavilion as idyll, to allow the illusion of idyllic life. The pavilion in an enclave in a domain; that is important in this story; not the formal solutions which are very personal and already history.

173

174

175

176

177

Noon, 20 November
1985, Copenhagen
Airport, Kastrup,
PS.

Of all pieces of furniture, the chair is most able to carry, like some portable shrine, the essence of the style of its period.

'The Chair', written
for Tecta's
Stuhlmuseum, Burg
Beverungen,
catalogue Der
Kragstuhl, published
1986.

People rarely collect cupboards or dressing tables or stools, but to collect chairs is common: it is probable that we see them as domestic pets – they have legs, feet, arms, backs; they are symmetrical in one direction; like animals, like ourselves.

The act of making territory starts with our clothes, with their style and with our gestures and postures when we wear them. With a chair we extend our sense of territory beyond our skin. With a chair we first impose ourselves on blind space.

It could be said that when we design a chair we make a society and a city in the small. Certainly this has never been more obvious than in this century. One has a perfectly clear notion of the sort of city and the sort of society envisaged by Mies van der Rohe , even though he has never said much about it. It is not an exaggeration to say that the Miesian city is implicit in the Mies chair.°

When we design a chair we make a society and a city in the small: Mies van der Rohe, el Lisitzky, Rietveld, Le Corbusier, Marcel Breuer, Jean, Prouvé, Charles and Ray Eames, A and P Smithson; the Bench of Judges, the Seat of Government, the Chairman of the Board, the Chair of Mechanical Engineering, the Throne of the King, the Heavenly Throne.

° From Team 10
Primer, edited by
AS, Studio Vista,
London, and MIT
Press, Cambridge,
Mass., 1968.

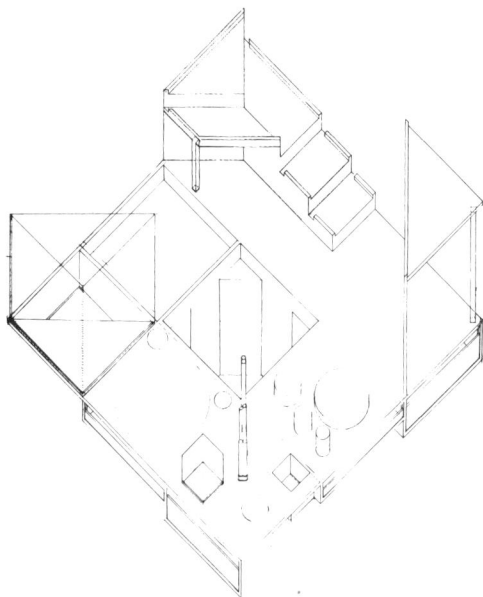

178

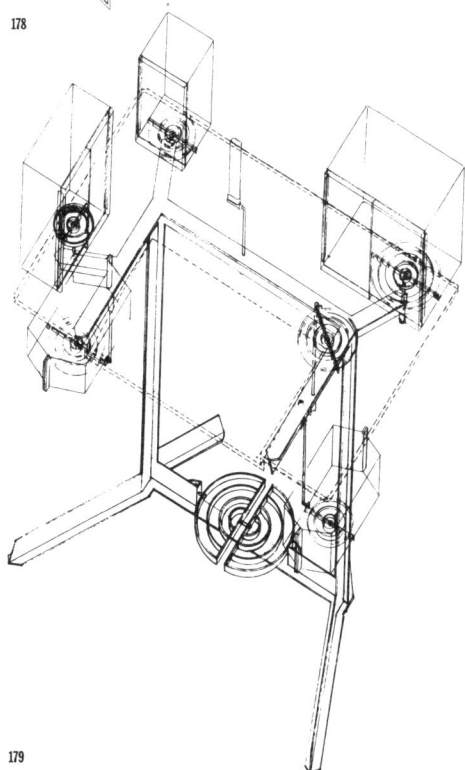

179

4 November 1986
AS.

'Collector's Table'
and 'Waterlily/Fish
Desk', descriptive
material in Tecta
catalogues, late
1980s.

The Collector's Table and the Waterlily/Fish Desk[178, 179] represent a move away from our generation's attitude to display and furniture in general. This was one of against the wall, which meant, in effect, forming the shelf wall or tucking shelves into alcoves and thereby re-proportioning and smoothing out the profile of the room into as near acceptable rectangles as possible. We inherited much of this from the previous generation's interest in the minimal space which became particularly pertinent in post-war socialist times in which, even if you did not have these interests as an ideology, everyone tended to, or was obliged to, frugally inhabit whatever spaces came their way.

In the 1990s our aspirations – always changing – are burgeoning and many people wish to inhabit liberally. We can therefore think again of furniture as occupying positions in our spaces rather than backed against a wall. Furniture for all functions – not only chairs or settees grouped for high or low tables – can take position in space to display collectors' pieces: the Collector's Table.[180]

The free-standing thought liberated the programme of years for a writing desk: a box for paper; a box for envelopes and cards; a box for the dictionary, thesaurus, address book; drawers, that by turning offer four front ends for pens, clips; and, as an aid to thinking what to write, a base to pedal with both feet – the Waterlily/Fish Desk.[181]

The choice of colours seem at variance in the two items of furniture; yet are not so.

The finish on the Collector's Table is a move away from the basic colours of the Heroic Period of the Modern Movement that have been returned to repeatedly since the 1920s; basic colours that any collector might find not only difficult to integrate in his room but also find unreceptive to many of the objects he wants to display. The splatter-on-silver brings the lacquered surface happily to cohabit with natural woods, marbles, and so on.

In the Waterlily/Fish Desk the metallic lustre of the pedal base, the neutral, see-through writing surface, play this cohabitation role. Still in keep-

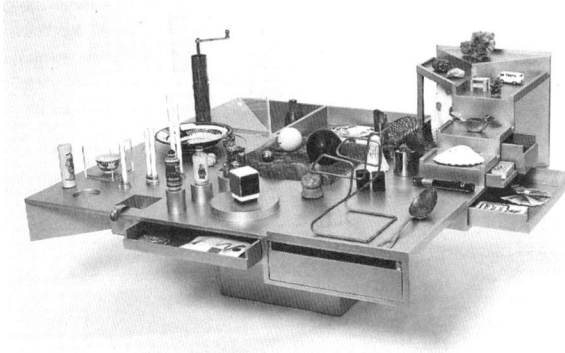

180

ing with our integrative thinking of the second half of the 1980s, the colours of the boxes might mutate within their language of waterlily above the water of the desk plane and fish below: time and personal need will tell.

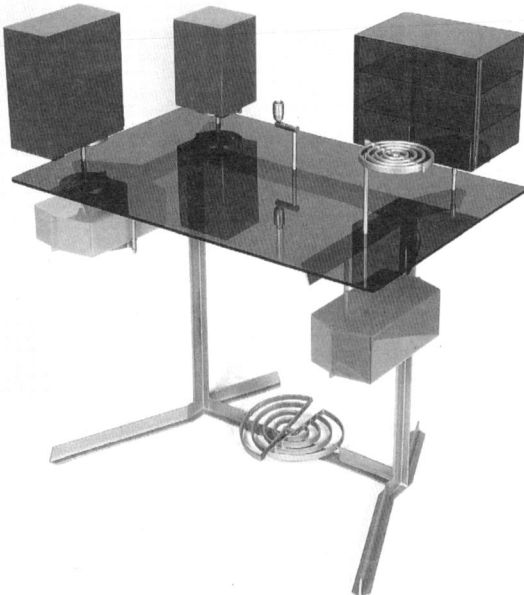

181

January 1987, AS.
Verbal illustration 1
to 'Collector's Table'
and 'Waterlily/Fish
Desk'.

The main attractions in the homes of the generation starting out in the 1950s were the new items
of ephemera. The world over, you would find virtually the same collection of travel memorabilia.

Both the Collector's Table and the Waterlily/Fish
Desk have come out of this same larder of objects
as intellectual food that fed our 1950s generation;
goodies which the Eames made banquet. But,
already rising in the late 1950s, was the English
interest in Victoriana; lace, feathers, wash-stands,
wash-bowls, retrieved from the family attic or out-
house; making the generation of the 1970s and
the 1980s collectors perhaps as never before.
Thus the shops of our large cities in the late 1980s
reflect both these fields of interest.

Verbal illustration 2
to 'Collector's Table'
and 'Waterlily/Fish
Desk'.

When an architect's mind takes a certain set with regard to spatial ordering it manifests itself in all the work of the period and can be seen earliest in the transient and small easily fabricated works.

From 'Conglomerate
Ordering'. See
Italian Thoughts,
Sweden, 1993.

Appendix 1 to 'Three
Pavilions'.
July 1986, AS.

In Aachen, to answer a question: 'What message 'Domain'.
does the Barcelona Pavilion hold for the future?', Unpublished.
PS made his statement about domain, relating it
not only to AS's paper at Aachen which generated
the question, but also to AS's Barcelona lecture
'Three Pavilions', and thus to the subject of the
seminar held by AS in Barcelona: 'Fragment of an
Enclave', the equivalent for the late 1980s of the
Barcelona Pavilion.

The definition of enclave was given as: 'The
piece of territory that can support and become the
mid- to late-1980s equivalent to the idyll of the
restorative-place-in-nature, that for the last two
centuries has taken the form of pavilion within
the landscaped park.'

The total retreat, the desert, where the person is
wholly reliant on the supportive environment; the place
away from it all: the idyll without any classical dressing, but with an overpowering sense of obtaining the
alternative society at all costs; the environment
allowed mastery over the man. The study/cell sort of
place, supportable only in an institution devoted to
study, in a society willing and able to support such
places as monasteries and colleges; a cell fully supported in its basic luxuries of seclusion and quiet and
freedom from interruption … quite often found in
urban locations because of the supports available.

The integrity of the pavilion relies on enough
money to give its fragment of an enclave protection within the greater territory of the domain.
Again, because of urban constraints, the integrity
is often best guaranteed – and for the longest dura-
tion – in an urban location.

In the 1990s the western idyll has implied within
in its dream, hidden, silent support systems (such
as supportive earning power).

We can specify the mundane and functional as
mechanisms that give time to the occupant to
enjoy his idyll, that are either virtually silent or
located so that the place – of study, of nature's
quiet – is not broken; natural energy being utilised
so that the pavilion has a sense of its support
being taken out of the air.

1 Mies van der Rohe: 860 Lake Shore Drive Apartments, Chicago, 1948–51. Detail view of corner at entrance level looking towards Lake Shore Drive, the lake beyond.

2, 3 Mies van der Rohe: 900 Esplanade Apartments, 880 and 860 Lake Shore Drive Apartments, Chicago, 1953–56 and 1948–51. General view with context (left) and at entrance level (right).

4, 5, 6 Mies van der Rohe: Illinois Institute of Technology, Chicago, 1939–58. View under the elevated railroad that passes through the campus to the Alumni Memorial Hall, 1956–46 (top); detail of early 1950s' skin (centre), and typical view on the IIT campus (bottom).

7, 8 Mies van der Rohe in association with Philip Johnson: Seagram Building, 375 Park Avenue, New York, 1954–58. Tear-sheet from The Architects' Journal, 28 April 1955, showing the model, and view during construction in 1957, showing the arrangement that binds the building to the cross-street on both sides.

9 Philip Johnson: The Glass House, New Canaan, Connecticut, 1949. View through the house to the landscape beyond.

10 Mies van der Rohe: 880 and 860 Lake Shore Drive Apartments, Chicago, 1948–51. General view looking towards Lake Shore Drive and the lake beyond.

11 Mies van der Rohe: Crown Hall, Illinois Institute of Technology, Chicago, 1950–56. General view of the main entrance.

12, 13 Mies van der Rohe: Commonwealth Promenade Apartments, Chicago, 1953–56. General view and detail of corner, looking up.

14 Mies van der Rohe: Promontory Apartments, Chicago, 1946–49. General view from the street.

15, 16 Mies van der Rohe (with Pace Associates): Carman Hall, Illinois Institute of Technology, Chicago, 1951–53. Carman Hall lies on the other side of the elevated railroad from the IIT campus proper. Its reinforced-concrete columns set-back towards the top of the building (as do those of the Promontory Apartments). Below: the entrance colonnade in high summer.

17, 18, 19 Mies van der Rohe: Lafayette Park, Detroit, master plan 1955–56, built 1958–63. Threshold and skin details of two-storey house (left); car-park in a one- and two-storey group (top right); flat-on detail of a two-storey house (bottom right).

20, 21, 22 Mies van der Rohe: municipal housing in the Afrikanischestrasse, Berlin, 1926–27. View from the street (top); 'flat-on' view of entry and window arrangement (centre); detail of basement window lintel and area grille (bottom).

23, 24 Mies van der Rohe: Hugo Perls House, Berlin-Zehlendorf, 1911. View from the street (top); detail of cornice and upper-floor windows (below).

25 Karl Friedrich Schinkel: The Altes Museum, 1824. Ground-floor plan.

26 Mies van der Rohe: Apartment Building, Weissenhofsiedlung, Stuttgart, 1927. A regular skin, fixed stair and services' locations, with varying room arrangements – Mies' standard apartment-house arrangement.

27 Mies van der Rohe: Factory for the Silk Industry, Krefeld, 1933. General view of single-storey factory building.

28, 29, 30 Mies van der Rohe: Lemcke House, Berlin, 1932. View from the street, and from the garden; detail of windows to garden – it is a surprisingly tall house.

31 Mies van der Rohe: Lafayette Park, Detroit, master plan 1955, built 1958–63. Single-storey houses with apartments behind.

32 Restored stoa of Attulus II of Pergamon, Athens; original construction c 140 BC. View along the colonnade.

33 The church of San Giovanni Fuorcivitas, Pistoia, begun in the twelfth century, completed in the fourteenth century. View of the street façade.

34 The Duomo, Orvieto, begun 1290. View along the platform on the north side.

35 The Procuratie Vecchie, Venice, rebuilt at the beginning of the sixteenth century. 'the front … is a copy of the old one (twelfth century) with an extra storey added, brought up to date only in the details' (McAndrew). Flat-on view from the Piazza San Marco.

36, 37 Mies van der Rohe: Colonnade Apartments, Colonnade Park, Newark, 1958–60. General view in context (above); detail of skin at corner (below).

38, 39 Mies van der Rohe: Metals and Minerals Research Building, Illinois Institute of Technology, Chicago, 1942–43. Typical junctions, steelwork to other components. (This was the first building by Mies van der Rohe to be erected in the USA.)

40 Mies van der Rohe: Concrete Office Building, 1922. Perspective drawing, charcoal and Conté crayon on brown paper. (Photograph courtesy Museum of Modern Art, New York.)

41 Mies van der Rohe: Factory for the Silk Industry, Krefeld, 1933. The arrangment of building and grounds is the forerunner for that of the IIT campus.

42, 43 Mies van der Rohe: The Farnsworth House, Plano, Illinois, 1945–50. Column between the upper (house) and lower (landing) platforms and view along the entrance platform on the Fox River side at the time of its original patron's occupation (photograph taken in 1958).

44, 45 Mies van der Rohe: Illinois Institute of Technology, Chicago, 1939-58. General view of the campus; the elevated railroad with Carman Hall beyond is to the right (above); a court on the campus (below).

46 The Farnsworth House. View from the side away from the river; it is a surprisingly big house, raised six or seven feet to the main house platform.

47 Mies van der Rohe: The Barcelona Pavilion, Barcelona, original construction 1928–29, demolished and subsequently rebuilt in its original location 1985. View across the platform during rebuilding.

48 The Farnsworth House. View from the house platform to the river bank over the landing platform.

49 Charles and Ray Eames: The Eames' House, Santa Monica, 1949. View along the 'meadow' towards the ocean, the line of eucalyptus trees on the right.

50 Alison and Peter Smithson: Upper Lawn, Tisbury, Wiltshire, 1959–82. The yard in winter, with 'Sun Man' by Eduardo Paolozzi.

51 The Eames' House. The view over the Pacific from the end of the Eames' House 'meadow'.

52, 53, 54, 55, 56 Upper Lawn. General view, fully open on the secluded side, with the Fonthill Woods beyond; 'The Great Snow' of 1987, with the Fonthill Woods beyond; activities of the yard in winter; activities of the yard in summer; the grass within the walls in high summer.

57 Leo von Klenze: the Königsplatz, Munich; Pynacothek 1848, Proplylaeum 1862, Glyptothek 1830. View towards the Propylaea. The floor of the in-between space, paved in the Nazi period, was originally gravel.

58, 59, 60, 61 The Barcelona Pavilion. Looking through the Pavilion to the entrance stair during rebuilding; travertine walls, bench and platform surrounding the 'open' tank during rebuilding; marble cladding on the outside of the north wall around the 'enclosed' tank during rebuilding.

62 The Barcelona Pavilion. View into the open-at-the-top slot during the rebuilding period (1985). In the rebuilt version the completed slot has a transparent cover.

63 The Barcelona Pavilion. Travertine walls, bench and platform surrounding the 'open' tank on completion of the rebuilding.

64 The Königsplatz. Bench on the Pynacothek side of the platz: detail with figures.

65 Mies van der Rohe (consulting architect): Dominion Center, Toronto, 1963–69. A space set apart.

66 The Barcelona Pavilion. 'The predictable path'.

67 Mies van der Rohe: Library and Administration Building, Illinois Institute of Technology, Chicago, 1944. Perspective drawing of a corner. (Drawing from The Architects' Journal, 3 January 1946.)

68 The Barcelona Pavilion. Interior view towards the 'open' pool during rebuilding.

69 The Barcelona Pavilion. 'King Alfonso XIII and Mies van der Rohe in the German Pavilion the day it was opened, 27 May 1929'. (Photograph courtesy Public Foundation for the Mies van der Rohe German Pavilion in Barcelona.)

70 The Barcelona Pavilion. Plan from Philip Johnson's book on Mies van der Rohe, originally published in 1947. (Drawing courtesy Museum of Modern Art, New York.)

71 The Barcelona Pavilion. View from the back where the ground is level with the platform of the pavilion. (Photograph courtesy Quaderns, October/November/December 1984.)

72 The Barcelona Pavilion. View of the exit leading to the higher ground: on the roof can be seen the transparent cover to the rectangular 'slot' – which does not seem to give any light.

73 Alison and Peter Smithson: Lucas Headquarters, Solihul, 1979. Aerial perspective with trees showing interior of spaces. (Drawing by Lorenzo Wong and Alison Smithson).

74, 75 Thomas Jefferson: Monticello, near Charlottesville, 1769–1809. View across the lawn to the west front of the house; the balustrade of the terrace can be seen on top of the south-side service wing and the out-house (top); view from the terrace west to the countryside (below).

76, 77, 78 Aachen. Flemish house near the Dom; the Dom (8th century onwards; Gothic choir, 1353–1413); Flemish houses.

79 Karl Friedrich Schinkel: Eisenbrunnen Colonnade, Aachen. A stoa form giving access to a thermal drinking fountain.

80 Charlemaigne's Throne in the Dom at Aachen.

81 Mies van der Rohe: Mr Chair with arms, 1926. Working drawing (?), original at 1:1 scale. (Photograph courtesy of Museum of Modern Art, New York.)

82 W Baren, Tietz Warehouse, Leipzigerstrasse, Berlin, 1896. Observation from a book in the possession of Heinz Rauch, Wupertal. (Drawing by Alison Smithson.)

83, 84, 85 H P Berlage: The Gemeentemuseum, The Hague, 1919–1935. (Top) on the left the flank of the entrance walkway, with the bulk of the museum behind; (below left) windows on the side of the main building; (below right) window to the boiler house.

86 Conservatory in the Summer Palace, Makasar, Bukhara (built by Russian engineers).

87 Alison and Peter Smithson: Hunstanton Secondary Modern School, 1950–54. Reflections of the sky in the glass on the south side during construction.

88 Mies van der Rohe. Assumed to have been taken inside 860 Lake Shore Drive near its completion around 1951 when Mies van der Rohe would have been 65 years old.

89 Le Corbusier's 'Geometric Solids' from Vers une architecture (1923). Part of the tail-piece of the chapter called 'The lesson of Rome'. (Reproduced from the translation, Towards a New Architecture, Architectural Press, London, 1927 and 1946.)

90 Le Corbusier's arrangement of glasses, bottles and plates. From New World of Space, Ler Corbusier, Reynal & Hitchcock, New York, 1948.

91 Jeanneret (Le Corbusier), painting, 1919, oil on canvas. From New World of Space, Le Corbusier, Reynal & Hitchcock, New York, 1948.

92, 93 The Eames House. The south end of the house facing towards the Pacific Ocean (top); two brooms and a rake against the house wall to the patio between house and studio (bottom).

94 Charles and Ray Eames: House of Cards Picture Deck; 1952.

An arrangement of the cards.

95, 96 Charles and Ray Eames: Wire Mesh Chair, 1951–53. Wire chair with 'Eiffel Tower' base: front and side elevations (above); plan and detail of chromium-plated 'Eiffel Tower' base supporting a plastic shell (below). (Photographs from John and Marilyn Neuhardt, Eames Design, Thames & Hudson, 1989, and Architectural Design, September 1966.)

97 Wire Mesh Chair, 1951–53. An assembly of black wire chairs and the famous backbird. (Architectural Design, September 1966.)

98 Courrèges clothes, 1967. Cover of Collections '67, Voici Courrèges.

99,100 Charles and Ray Eames: Aluminium Group Chairs, 1958. Details of seat side ribs (above) and 'antler' frame under (below).

101 The Eames' House. The house and the studio beyond, seen from the 'meadow' through the line of eucalyptus trees.

102 Alison Smithson: a set of three 'Economist' red boxes, 1963. Dressing table (or make-up box); sideboard; drinks cabinet.

103 Roorkee chair (bought at the Army and Navy Stores) in the yard at Upper Lawn. Upper Lawn is in its opened-up state for the high summer, the Roorkee chair moved into the yard.

104,105 Alison and Peter Smithson, Priory Walk, London, 1971–71. Top-floor general living room decorated for Christmas (above); kitchen equipment in the same room.

106 Charles and Ray Eames: plastic armchair with 'Eiffel Tower' base (front), 1950–53; wire mesh chair with 'Eiffel Tower' base and two-piece leather pad (back), 1951–53. The two chairs on the pavement outside 46 Limerston Street, Chelsea.

107 The Eames' House. Diagram of a possible façade pattern (drawing by Charles and Ray Eames).

108 Upper Lawn. Harvesting completed; Fonthill Woods in the background.

109 The Eames' studio workshop, 901 Washington Boulevard, Venice, California. A former automobile repair shop used as studio/workshop by the Eames from 1943 onwards. (Charles Eames used the term 'shop' generally to describe one's place of work.)

110 The Eames House. Reflections of the line of eucalyptus trees seen from the boardwalk serving front yard/house/patio/studio/back yard.

111 A child's gift to Ray Eames.

112 Helene Weigel as Mother Courage in the 1949 production of Mother Courage and Her Children at the Deutscher Theater, Berlin. (Photograph by Eric Bentley.)

113 Upper Lawn. Flat-on view of turkey-bush on wall with red currants.

114 The Eames House. Chair with 'Eiffel Tower' base, guarded by the blackbird.

115 The Flexible Flyer. Plan and side elevation of the classic American toboggan. (Measured and drawn by Simon Smithson.)

116, 117, 118 Challenge steel windmill in Coryell Country, Texas (top). The windmill's vane has been blown to the ground. Ozark vaneless windmill (below). A windmill abandoned in a pasture in Ford du Lac County, Wisconsin. Iron turbine windmill (right). On exhibit at the Sharlot Hall Historical Museum, Prescott, Arizona. (Photographs from T Lindsay Baker, A Field Guide to American Windmills, University of Oklahoma Press, 1985.)

119 House of Cards Picture Deck.

120, 121 Nigel Henderson, Eduardo Paolozzi, Alison and Peter Smithson: 'Patio and Pavilion', This is Tomorrow exhibition, Whitechapel Art Gallery, London, 1956. Reflections and objects within the patio (top); the pavilion within the patio, seen from above (bottom).

122 'Patio and Pavilion'. Tear-sheet of two pages from the catalogue. One-point perspective drawing by Peter Smithson, collage by Eduardo Paolozzi.

123 Alison and Peter Smithson: 'Patio and Pavilion', as rebuilt at the ICA, London, 1990. View up through the semi-transparent roof covering of displayed 'as-found' objects.

124 'Patio and Pavilion'. The ground within the patio.

125 Le Corbusier and Pierre Jeanneret with Charlotte Perriand, René Herbst and Signot: Exposition de Bruxelles, 1935. Storage cabinet. (Photograph from Le Corbusier, Oeuvre Complet, Zurich, 1945.)

126 Le Corbusier and Pierre Jeanneret with Charlotte Perriand: Salon d'Automne, 1929. Wardrobe in bedroom. (Photograph from Le Corbusier, Oeuvre Complet, Zurich, 1935.)

127 Le Corbusier and Pierre Jeanneret: Villa Savoye at

Poissy, 1929. The entrance hall. (Photograph from Le Corbusier, Oeuvre Complet, Zurich, 1935.)

128 Le Corbusier: Unité d'Habitation, Marseilles, 1946–53. Kitchen by Charlotte Perriand, seen from the stair by Jean Prouvé. (Photograph from Le Corbusier, L'Unité d'Habitation de Marseille, Le Point, 1950.)

129 'The Small Pleasures of Life'. Drawings by Alison Smithson, 1950s.

130 Alison and Peter Smithson: the Appliance House, 1957–58. Two diagrams showing the space organisation of a Western (right) and a Japanese house. In the latter, storage space is separated from the living area which flows freely through the house volume. (Drawing by Alison Smithson.)

131 Alison and Peter Smithson: the 'Snowball' Appliance House, 1957–58. A cluster group (top), entrance elevation and plans, 'open' and 'closed'. (Drawings by Alison Smithson.)

132 Alison and Peter Smithson: the 'Strip' Appliance House, 1957–58. Plan of a terrace of 'Strip' houses (left) and detail plan. (Drawing by Alison Smithson.)

133 'Strip' Appliance House. View of 'strip' screened by garages from parallel vehicular road (top); view along the area between 'strips' (with parking at the ends) (centre); an idea for a standard cubicle house with an extra ground-floor room with a separate entrance (see Churchill College Tutor's House and Master's Lodge). (Drawings by Alison Smithson.)

134 Alison and Peter Smithson: 'House of the Future', Ideal Homes Exhibition, London, 1956. 'Fougasse layout' (a fougasse is a type of French fancy bread with slits in it, more-or-less of the pattern of this drawing) – a typical arrangement, back-to-back, of the House of the Future. (Drawing by Peter Smithson.)

135 'House of the Future'. Diagramatic plans.

136 'House of the Future'. View into the kitchen from the living room.

137 'House of the Future'. Kitchen equipment and mobile food trolley seen through a viewing aperture cut into the external wall (exhibition visitors were not allowed inside the house). (Photograph: Council of Industrial Design.)

138 Alison and Peter Smithson: Villa at St Albans (System Rumble), 1954. A project using an already developed shuttering system to generate a new type of family home.

A possible group layout, 'the chain'. (Drawing by Alison Smithson.)

139 Villa at St Albans (System Rumble). Aplication of the shuttering system to a conventional single-family house location. (Drawing by Alison Smithson.)

140 Alison Smithson: the 'Bread' Appliance House, 1957. Sketch of group; and ground floor and alternative plans for the upper floor with sketches of the general form. (Drawings by Alison Smithson.)

141 Advertisement for Citroën ID DS 19, c 1960. From Bauen & Wohnen.

142, 143 Braun advertising from the 1960s. Tear-sheets from pamphlet advertising the L50 loudspeaker with Audio 1 radio and PL45 record player (top), and the T540 portable transistor radio (below). (Pamphlet from Wooland, Knightsbridge, London.)

144 Joe Colombo: 'Universale' chair, 1965. Side elevation. (Photograph from Ignazia Favata, Joe Colombo, Thames & Hudson, 1988.)

145 Southcot Place, Bath. Southcot Place is an open-cornered L, facing south uphill (the false double-hung sashes are a fairly rare formal device in Bath).

146 John Wood the Elder: South Parade, Bath, laid out 1738, built 1740–48. The pavement (raised above the river level, with useable spaces under) is 33 feet wide.

147, 148 Le Corbusier and Pierre Jeanneret: La Cité de Refuge par l'Armé du Salut, Paris, 1929–33. View of the entrance from the Rue Cantagrel: 'across a bridgeway to the circular vestibule' (top); view of the back of the porch 'of strictly cubic intention', from the Rue Cantagrel (below).

149 St Mary's Buildings, Bath. General view, with Camden Crescent on the far hillside.

150 Alison and Peter Smithson: Robin Hood Gardens, Tower Hamlets, London, 1966–72. Cotton Street Building from the churchyard gate of All Saints' with St Frideswide's Church. The walkways ('decks') can be understood, even from a distance.

151 Robin Hood Gardens. View over the protecting acoustic wall along Cotton Street of the external face with the upper walkway.

152 Robin Hood Gardens. View of the internal face from the central green space with the bedroom balconies opening on to this quiet garden.

153 Robin Hood Gardens. Typical bedroom facing towards the internal green space with the French windows open, (Photograph by Sandra Lousada.)

154 Robin Hood Gardens. The walkway outside the largest flats widens to offer a play-space for children. (Photograph by Sandra Lousada.)

155, 156, 157, 158 J J P Oud: 'De Kiefhoek' houses, Rotterdam, 1925. The stair handrail (top left); the landing handrail (top right); the street façade (bottom left); the façade to the back garden (bottom right).

159 Cité de Refuge. General view of the 'preparations for entry'. (Photograph from Le Corbusier et Pierre Jeanneret, Zurich, 1946.)

160 Santos-Dumont. At the controls of the Demoiselle (Collection Dazy). (Photograph from The Story of an Obsession, Wykham.)

161 Le Corbusier and Pierre Jeanneret: Immeuble 'Clarté', Geneva, 1930–32. Façade. (Photograph from Le Corbusier Oeuvre Complet, Zurich, 1946.)

162 Van Tijen, Brinkmann and Van der Vlugt: 'Bergpolder' flats, Rotterdam, 1933–34. Structural section and view from the north west. (From Alfred Roth, The New Architecture, Zurich, 1946.)

163 Jules Saulnier: Menier Chocolate Factory, Noisel-sur-Marne, 1871–72. Structural arrangement and elevation. (From Siegfried Giedion, Space, Time and Architecture, 1946.)

164, 165 Beaudouin and Lods with Jean Prouvé and Vladimir Bodiansky: Maison du Peuple, Clichy, 1937–39. Street view (top) and detail of street corner (below).

166 Gustave Eiffel: Viaduc de Garabit sur la Truyère, 1885–88. View up one of the piers.

167 Robin Hood Gardens. '… for the inhabitants to know without conscious thought where to offer their abilities …'. Girls playing in the central green space. (Photograph by Sandra Lousada.)

168 The Farnsworth House. View from the lawn behind the house as restored by Peter Palumbo, with Alison Smithson standing by the open platform.

169 The Eames House. The house seen from the 'meadow' through the line of eucalyptus trees.

170 Upper Lawn. '… layers added by the seasons and the occupier…': a layer of red-currants, a bird, a layer of snow.

171 Upper Lawn. The photographer (PS) reflected in the aluminium-sheet-faced door.

172 The Eames House. Chair with 'Eiffel Tower' base, guarded by the blackbird.

173 Upper Lawn. 'Bamboo in a box': view out south east to ancient earthwork fortification.

174 Upper Lawn. The house opened up for high summer.

175 Upper Lawn. Winter well: well head with cover stone. This stone took two adults to move if anyone wanted to see down the well.

176 Upper Lawn. The mulberry tree in the great snow of 1978.

177 Upper Lawn. Snow in the yard, with wood saws.

178 Alison Smithson: The Collector's Table (third version) 1986. Axonometric view from the lamp corner.

179 Alison Smithson: The Waterlily/Fish Writing Desk, 1986. Cut-away axonometric view from the writing side of the desk.

180 The Collector's Table, 1989. Table and collection, some drawers open. (Photograph: Tecta.)

181 The Waterlily/Fish Writing Desk, 1989. View from the writing side of the desk. (Photograph: Tecta.)